D1120208

D. W. Griffith

American Film Master

by Iris Barry

with an annotated list of films by Eileen Bowser

The Museum of Modern Art,

New York

Distributed by Doubleday & Company, Inc.,

Garden City, New York

Acknowledgments

On behalf of the Trustees of The Museum of Modern Art, I wish to thank The British Film Institute, The George Eastman House, The Hollywood Museum, and the Killiam-Sterling Collection for the loan of films while these notes were in preparation, and for the D. W. Griffith exhibition; Andrew C. McKay for help in checking names and dates; Richard Griffith for helpful suggestions in the manuscript.

E.B.

CONTENTS

Company shot during filming of SALLY OF THE SAWDUST, *1925 with W. C. Fields and D. W. Griffith in center.*

FOREWORD

As first curator of The Museum of Modern Art Film Library, Iris Barry was also the first to rediscover and re-examine the primitive films of the late nineteenth and early twentieth centuries, especially the series of short films made for the American Mutoscope and Biograph Company by D. W. Griffith between 1908 and 1913. How Miss Barry found them, salvaged them and restored a considerable number of them to the screen is a story which has been told elsewhere. What is perhaps not on record, what even this book does not altogether communicate, is this pioneering curator's growing excitement as she found from personal experience that Griffith had in four short years discovered and laid down *all* the basic principles of the multiform twentieth-century medium which Robert Gessner has called the art of the moving image. It was a triumph for The Museum of Modern Art to uncover this fact. The origins of the older arts are lost in prehistory, their creators unknown or barely guessed at. Here was almost the complete record of the birth of an art—and its leading artist, though he had been inactive for a decade, was still alive!

The Museum, in keeping with its general outlook and policy, immediately set out to communicate this discovery. In 1940, a large exhibition of the Griffith films then available and the artifacts connected with them was held in the new Museum building. As a pendant to the Griffith film series, Miss Barry wrote and the Museum published the study that follows. It was based on her unique knowledge of the films themselves, on exhaustive conversations with Griffith, and on a stay in Louisville which produced the brief but magical vignette of a Kentucky childhood and youth which goes so far to explain his later development and history.

She hoped to restore the fading fame of this "enigmatic and somewhat tragic figure," as Gilbert Seldes had called him, and also to overcome the long-lived intellectual prejudice which held (at least by implication) that because Griffith worked for vast audiences and made (and lost) a great deal of money, his achievement could not be classed with "real" art. The experiment was not an unqualified success. Outside the then tiny circle of film scholars the book provoked little cerebration and comment, and it did not sell; overstocks remained on the Museum's shelves for years. In 1940 Griffith and his era seemed fantastically remote and irrelevant to most people who thought of themselves as cultivated. His spotty knowledge of history, his literary eccentricities, his "petit bourgeois" morality quite overshadowed for them the beauty, power and humanity of his formal structure and pictorial composition. If this was, indeed, the art of the motion picture, as Miss Barry insisted, then they were not much interested—primarily, in this writer's opinion, because it did not look or sound much like the art with which they were familiar and at ease. Novelty in any undertaking, it seems, is either cultivated for novelty's sake or is automatically regarded as anathema; it tends to obscure more lasting values which only time can bring out.

Time has certainly given Griffith his revenge. Today, the youngest film student is as familiar with THE NEW YORK HAT and A CORNER IN WHEAT as the student of English is with *Beowulf* and *Piers Plowman,* largely through the Museum's educational showings and circulation of these and other Griffith films. The rediscovery, or re-rediscovery, of Griffith's mastery has even extended to television. Every maker of films automatically acknowledges his debt to Griffith, as part, it would seem, of a sort of ceremony of initiation into the circle of fame. And *D. W. Griffith: American Film Master,* so long a drug on the market, has been out of print for years and is recognized as a valuable collector's item throughout the world.

It is now again the Museum's agreeable task to extend and refine the growing knowledge of Griffith's life and work with a large exhibition of his work, including seventeen films that were not available for the Film Library's 1940 showing (at least one of them, TRUE HEART SUSIE, a master creation). Miss Barry's monograph, presented here as it originally appeared, and Beaumont Newhall's essay, updated by him in light of new information, are republished in connection with the exhibition. Miss Barry's original text has been supplemented by a long addendum by Eileen Bowser, based on material only recently available for scholarly use. As Director of the Griffith exhibition, Mrs. Bowser has studied at length the films included in it as well as many others not yet prepared for public exhibition. She has also, through the generosity of The Rockefeller Foundation, spent more than a year preparing an annotated catalog of the vast collection of D. W. Griffith's personal and business papers and other memorabilia, to be published by the Museum in the near future. While Miss Barry and her assistant, Katherine Stone, had access to these papers when they arrived at the Museum in 1939, they were then in a state of considerable confusion, and it was not until Mrs. Bowser finished her long study that the Griffith record could really be read. The correlation of seemingly isolated situations and individuals, the reconciling of discordant facts and figures, and the interweaving of all the complicated data of a complicated life into a single skein is her great contribution to our understanding of Griffith's career and fate.

Richard Griffith
Curator, Film Library

D. W. Griffith:
American Film Master by Iris Barry

When Fanny Ward returned to the stage in 1907, she first appeared in James K. Hackett's Washington production of *A Fool and a Girl,* a short-lived play by David Wark Griffith, an almost unknown author who was destined for world fame within the next decade, though in another medium. The *New York Telegraph,* reporting next day on this drama of San Francisco low life and the California hopfields, mentioned that the playwright had some reputation as a short-story writer. He had published a free-verse poem in *Leslie's Weekly* a few months before. The previous May in Boston, upon the occasion of his first marriage, he had described himself as thirty years old, a writer by profession, and a resident of Louisville, Kentucky.

By 1907, however, a career of ten years as an actor already lay behind him. It had been followed under a pseudonym. Though as a writer he signed his full and proper name, he apparently felt that the other activities he had engaged in in a rather disheartening struggle for existence might reflect adversely upon his family. So it was as Lawrence Griffith that he had become an actor in Louisville, making his debut at a charity performance, then faring forth with a troupe of local entertainers[1] and, finally, after an earlier unsuccessful attempt, he joined the Meffert Stock Company. Here at the Masonic Temple Theatre, Griffith appeared twice a day in supporting roles through the season of 1897–98 and again, briefly, at the end of 1898–99 season. Louisville residents still speak affectionately of the old Temple Theatre, long since destroyed by fire. Matrons who attended it as girls recall that they secretly entertained a romantic passion for the company's leading man, Oscar Eagle. But local recollection of the tall young fellow who appeared now as the footman in *Little Lord Fauntleroy,* as Parker Serrant in *Lady Windermere's Fan,* or as Athos in *The Three Guardsmen* is not particularly vivid.

The nineties were in their full glory then, with the theatre —as it no longer is now—an absorbing and vital part of the social and intellectual life of the nation. Intensely musical and theatre-conscious Louisville, for instance, supported at that time not only the Temple Theatre, the Auditorium (for major attractions like Sousa's Band or Sarah Bernhardt), the Avenue Theatre (melodrama and buckets of blood), the Buckingham Theatre (burlesque), the Bijou Theatre (variety), but also the justly famous Macauley's Theatre, which, for long years, drew to itself the greatest of stage celebrities from all over the world. Here Mary Anderson made her debut and here Modjeska produced the first Ibsen play in the United States.

Here, too, the young Griffith, from the gallery, had seen Julia Marlowe in *Romeo and Juliet* and forthwith determined to become an actor and a dramatist. He could glimpse from afar local celebrities coming over after dinner at the Pendennis Club to greet their acquaintances in the boxes and parquet of the large horseshoe-shaped theatre, strolling out between acts to visit the stars backstage or dropping in at the Crockford to enjoy "one fried oyster or sausage with each drink, except a schooner." But Griffith, by reason of his youth and poverty, stood on the outer fringes of all this gaiety, as he did too of less decorous amusements which the pleasant city offered—concert halls like Beirod's with its lively orchestra and ambulant hostesses, and the innumerable establishments on Green Street where, in one back room at least, a colored pianist, strayed upriver from New Orleans or Memphis, was already strumming out a strange ragtime rhythm of his own. "Jerry played everything with that chop beat," a contemporary recalls. "But we were more concerned with the harpist in the Temple Theatre orchestra. After the show we used to load him and his harp on to a cab and go round serenading our sweethearts." Meanwhile Griffith had been taking singing lessons and attending the Methodist Sunday School. Buying tickets for the theatre, before he became an actor, must have entailed quite a sacrifice.

The boy's background was one familiar enough, of high traditions, past glories and present straits. His paternal great-grandfather, Salathiel Griffith, deputy-constable and sheriff of Somerset County, Maryland, was a considerable citizen[2] of the young republic. His grandfather, Daniel Weatherby Griffith (presumably Salathiel's youngest son) resided in Charlestown, Jefferson County, Virginia,[3] but in 1840, twice widowed, moved on west to Kentucky where his twenty-year-old son, Jacob Wark Griffith, seems already to have settled. Property had also come to them through Daniel Griffith's first wife, Margaret Wark. Jacob Griffith studied and practiced medicine in Kentucky, fought at Buena Vista and Saltillo in the Mexican War, and went west as captain-escort of one of the innumerable wagon-trains leaving Missouri for California in 1850. During the session of 1853–54 he was a member of the Kentucky legislature. In 1848 he had married Mary Perkins Oglesby, a member of the Carter clan of Virginia. A son who lived but a few months, a daughter, a son, and another daughter had been born on the Griffith place near Crestwood, Oldham County, Kentucky, before the outbreak of the Civil War found Captain Jacob in command of Company E., First Kentucky Cavalry, C.S.A. Soon promoted to lieutenant-colonel of the second organization, he was severely wounded at Hewey's Bridge and at Sequatchie Valley. Late in 1863, the Colonel's figure loomed picturesquely through national history when—badly wounded for the third time and unable to walk—he commandeered a horse

6

MEFFERT STOCK COMPANY. 1897-8

Thomas Reynolds,   Wm. Blackmore,   Lawrence Griffith,   Oscar Eagle,   Edmond Day,   Adolph Lestiner,   Arthur Livingston,
Anna McGregor,   Lila Jeanette Howel, Beatrice Ingram,   Col. Wm. H. Meffert, Esther Lyon,   Sara Cameron,   Josephine Sejournant

"Lawrence" Griffith, third from left at back, with the Meffert Stock Company, Louisville, Kentucky 1897–98.

and buggy and in it led his regiment to a victorious charge. His great booming voice had already earned him the soubriquet of "Roaring Jake" Griffith.[4] Surrendering to the victorius North at Irwinsville, Georgia, on May 10, 1865, after vainly attempting to escort President Davis westward to safety, he returned to the home which his wife—like so many other wives—had been struggling to keep going through the years of conflict.

The Griffith place at Crestwood no longer stands: a newer farmhouse was built on its site in 1911 and recently the last of the tall cedars round the old house and all of the avenue of trees running up to it, a full quarter of a mile from the La Grange-Louisville turnpike, have been cut down. It was probably never a "great" house, certainly the land was never very rich: hazards of war raging back and forth across neutral Kentucky impoverished it further. By the time of David Wark Griffith's birth on January 23, 1875, a few months before the first Kentucky Derby, the constant struggle with poverty had become acute. Colonel Griffith, again elected to the Lower House from his district in 1878, seems, from the kindly reports of surviving relatives, to have been something of a visionary, and improvident. At any rate, after his death in 1885 it appeared that he had been paying ten per cent compound interest on several mortgages: there was less than nothing left.

7

Cashboy, Journalist, Trouper

D. W. Griffith's earliest and psychologically quite interesting memory is of attending a magic-lantern show in the village school along with his father, for whom he preserves an almost idolatrous admiration. But later memories are of driving cows home through a menacing dusk, of bullies at the local school, of riding into Louisville atop a cart laden with the family's sole remaining possessions when, in his teens, poverty had driven the widow and younger children from their birthplace to an even more pinched farm and, finally, into the city.

The boy Griffith helped out as best he could, now as cashboy in Lewis' Dry Goods Store, where he was embarrassed to be seen by more prosperous friends of his father's, now as errand boy in the Flexner bookstore. He seems also to have had jobs on the *Louisville Courier* and in a second dry goods store. Once he was a super at the Auditorium, probably when Sarah Bernhardt appeared in *Gismonda* and *The Lady of the Camellias* in 1896. But when he finally joined the Meffert Stock Company he brought with him to the eager performance of modest roles little more than a Southerner's sense of personal and tribal importance, a familiarity with Shakespeare and the Bible which he had heard read out loud each night by lamplight in the old home by the Colonel, his father, together with a resonant voice and diction of remarkable purity.

After leaving the Meffert Stock Company, "Lawrence" Griffith continued to be an actor with little pecuniary success, touring with a number of companies which commonly folded en route, leaving the cast stranded. By his own account,[5] he was almost penniless, frequently fired and often compelled to resort temporarily to other means of livelihood. The details of these years are not too clear. There was a period when he sold subscriptions to *The Baptist Weekly* and the *Encyclopaedia Britannica* in rural Kentucky. We know that he left Louisville for New York with $19 and secured a small part in a melodrama which expired in Tonawanda, New York, where he worked as an ore shoveler until he had the fare back to Broadway. Engaged at $25 a week in a *London Life* road company, he was stranded in Minneapolis and beat his way back to Louisville with difficulty. Again New York, flophouses, a construction job, then comparative success as a member of Ada Gray's company on her farewell tour in 1904, during which he played small roles in *Trilby* and in *East Lynne*. The same year we trace him in Chicago as Abraham Lincoln in *The Ensign* with the Neill Alhambra Stock Company, and the next year with the Melbourne MacDowell Company in *Fedora*. He was again stranded or fired in Portland, Oregon; worked his way up and down the coast on lumber schooners; picked hops; played in *The Financier* in San Francisco and in *Ramona* in Los Angeles; then joined

Nance O'Neill's *Elizabeth, Queen of England* as Sir Francis Drake. He toured with this company from January to May 1906, at which time, still with the same company, he appeared in *Rosmersholm* and *Magda* in Boston and there married Linda Arvidson Johnson, a young actress whom he had met the previous year in San Francisco. Still no great success blessed him, though James Hackett unexpectedly paid him $1,000 for *A Fool and a Girl*. But otherwise 1907 was a lean year, the failure of the play was undoubtedly a keen disappointment, and Griffith was compelled once more to look for employment outside the theatre. This time he tried something new—the motion pictures.

Movies were no longer a novelty, for they had established themselves as a public entertainment in 1895 and by now were fairly prevalent; but they had established themselves in amusement parlors or as the final, and expulsive, turn in variety shows, and they ranked little above a flea circus. Actors, particularly, had a huge contempt for them and for the people who played in them. This seems curious, since Joseph Jefferson had appeared in a series of the early mutoscopes and Sarah Bernhardt enacted the duel scene from *Hamlet* for the screen in 1900. The fact remained that even an obscure actor "at rest" regarded work in the movies as rather worse than death.

Now under financial compulsion Griffith set out on the round of the various film firms to try to sell ideas for film stories. At the Edison studio he saw Edwin S. Porter who, four years before, in THE LIFE OF AN AMERICAN FIREMAN and THE GREAT TRAIN ROBBERY, had laid down the basis for cinematic story-telling on which Griffith later was so eminently to build. Porter refused Griffith's offer of a scenario based on *La Tosca* but offered him the leading part in a film he was about to make—RESCUED FROM AN EAGLE'S NEST. Griffith accepted, reluctantly, and as this film has been preserved we are able to witness his screen debut at very nearly first hand. The style is still approximately that of THE GREAT TRAIN ROBBERY, with painted canvas exteriors alternating with real ones, simple action which called for no explanatory wordage, and all actors seen full length and moving for the most part horizontally as on the stage. Griffith, a fine figure of a man, gives a robust performance but his woodsman-hero and the other adult participants in this "Western" tale are not much more convincing than the eagle.

8

A Fool and a Girl, *a play written by Griffith and produced by James K. Hackett in Washington in 1907. Fanny Ward (center), Alison Skipworth and Frank Wunderlee. (Photo courtesy of the Theatre Collection, New York Public Library.)*

The screen debut of "Lawrence" Griffith in RESCUED FROM AN EAGLE'S NEST, *1907.*

Shortly afterward he presented himself at the old Biograph studio on 14th Street, again with plots for sale, and here met with more permanent success. He sold several stories, among them OLD ISAACS THE PAWNBROKER, which was filmed in March 1908, OSTLER JOE and AT THE CROSSROADS OF LIFE. In these last two he, no doubt still reluctantly, also acted—as he did, too, in THE MUSIC MASTER and WHEN KNIGHTS WERE BOLD. The price for a story was usually $15, and actors were paid $5 a day. The first Mrs. D. W. Griffith, who has left an account of this period in *When the Movies Were Young,* had also obtained work with Biograph as an actress but kept her relationship to "Lawrence" Griffith a secret. Soon he was a fixture at Biograph. In scanning the synopses of the films of that time as advertised in the Biograph bulletins, it is evident that he had much to contribute from the start, though as yet it was only a rather more complex and probable type of plot than had been customary.

Biograph had fallen on difficult days at the moment Griffith joined it. Created in the very infancy of the movies, the American Mutoscope and Biograph Company had at first provided keen competition to the Edison kinetoscope with its own variant of the peepshow known as the mutoscope, a series of cardboard pictures set in a wheel and flipped over by a crank. Next it provided a lively rival to the Edison films with its own variety of large-size motion pictures. These "Biographs" had started out famously in 1896 with a little railroad film, THE EMPIRE STATE EXPRESS, and with shots of presidential candidate McKinley. Its first roof-top studio thereafter produced an extremely remarkable series of short pictures which, after 1903, began to utilize more plot and less mere incident, after the model of THE GREAT TRAIN ROBBERY. In 1906, with the advent of suitable artificial illumination, the firm moved indoors to 11 East 14th Street, but at this period its productions seem to have been less successful. Rival firms were stealing the lead, and there had been much litigation over patent rights. By 1907 Biograph was selling fewer than twenty prints of its subjects, and the employees were worried. The advent of Griffith into the firm rapidly proved to be extreme good fortune.

Griffith's companions in the studio noticed that he was a "human short-circuit type"; his energy and initiative soon earned him the chance to direct a picture, THE ADVENTURES OF DOLLIE, a little story which bore some resemblance to the English-made success of a few years earlier, RESCUED BY ROVER. The cameraman was to be Arthur Marvin, brother of the firm's general manager H. N. Marvin, but some instruction in the art of direction was volunteered to the novice by the firm's other photographer, G. W. "Billy" Bitzer, who had joined the firm in 1896 as an electrician. "The cameraman was the whole works at that time," Bitzer writes, "re-

sponsible for about everything except the immediate handling of the actors. It was his say not only as to whether the light was bright enough but make-up, angles, rapidity of gestures, etc., besides having enough camera troubles of his own. . . . I agreed to help him [Griffith] in every way. He needed a canvas covering for a gypsy wagon. I would get that, in fact all the props. Also I offered to condense the script and lay out the opportunities it had so that he would be able to understand it. . . . He came to my house a few evenings later. He had been out looking for a suitable location, wanted a swift, running stream quite close to a house. I had divided off half a dozen columns on the back of a laundry shirt-cardboard and headed the columns with titles —Drama, Comedy, Pathos, Pretty Scenes—and wrote in what I thought he should stress. . . . Judging the little I had caught from seeing his acting I didn't think he was going to be so hot. He was very grateful for this and some other tips I gave him. All through the following sixteen years that I was at his side he always was not above taking advice, yes, even asking for suggestions or ideas. He always said to me, 'Four eyes are better than two.' "

Trade advertisement for the first film directed by Griffith.

D. W. Griffith as a film actor with Marion Leonard in AT THE CROSSROADS OF LIFE, *1908.*

A CORNER IN WHEAT, *1909.*

Early Successes

Thus began one of the most remarkable associations in the history of the motion picture and thus inconspicuously did "the Master" enter upon his career. THE ADVENTURES OF DOLLIE was an immediate success and from then on Griffith, with Marvin or Bitzer behind the camera, worked at film-making for fourteen hours a day. Sales bounded up. The studio on 14th Street had space for only one set at a time but, though it is true that the finished films never exceeded one reel by more than a few feet and the total footage shot was never more than 1,600 (usually it was well under 1,000), it is astonishing how very many films were turned out. Apparently *all* Biograph films from June 1908 until December 1909 were made by Mr. Griffith, and all the important ones thereafter until 1913, at the rate of one twelve-minute and one six-minute subject every week. It is an amazing bulk, of amazing variety, but even more amazing is its liveliness and the vitality with which this newcomer's work developed.

While The Museum of Modern Art Film Library has been fortunate in obtaining all that remained of the Biograph product and papers, much of the film had already perished beyond recovery. There were few prints, and those

mostly in poor condition, while all too many of the negatives were in a state of disintegration, chemical action or moisture having quite ruined them. Moreover, the Biograph films of the period under review were made on stock with only two sprocket holes, so that it is impossible to make prints from such negatives on modern printing machines. It was only through the painstaking efforts of a member of the Film Library's staff, Mr. William Jamison (long associated with the Edison Company), that a means was found of obtaining prints from such of the negatives as were still in fair or good condition. He salvaged and practically remanufactured an old printing machine for the task. Mr. G. W. Bitzer likewise lent his extraordinary resourcefulness and experience to the adaptation of an original Biograph camera so that it might be used as a projector. This is most helpful for the examination of negatives and obviated the expense of making up prints of the many subjects to be examined. It is thanks to these two tireless pioneers that it has finally been possible for us to restore at least some of the early work of Mr. Griffith to the screen. Even so, the first two films he directed are lost and the earliest one recovered, THE BLACK VIPER, is not especially interesting.

Griffith's early work was of such quality, however, and pleased the public so well that on August 17, 1908, the firm signed him up at $50 a week, plus a guaranteed weekly commission of not less than $50. Between this date and his second contract[6] with Biograph in 1909 he made a hundred and thirty-one films and he completed another hundred before his third contract[7] in 1910 and a further ninety-five before the fourth contract[8] in 1911. Whereas the first two contracts were made out to Lawrence Griffith it is interesting to note that Lawrence is altered to David in pen in the third contract and that the fourth contract is made out directly to David Wark Griffith. Knowing how Griffith felt about the use of his real name, we can deduce that the degree of success and self-expression which attended his efforts had by now reconciled him to working in motion pictures. And well it might, for single-handed he was forging a new medium of expression out of them.

Edwin S. Porter in THE GREAT TRAIN ROBBERY had taken a vital step by introducing parallel action through a rough form of crosscutting, thus introducing a radically cinematic method of telling a story quite unlike the stage-bound method employed earlier. Porter had discovered the film's ability to juggle with time and space or to follow a continuity unlike that of normal experience.

Technical Innovations

Griffith, starting with Porter's method as still employed in RESCUED FROM AN EAGLE'S NEST, set out to improve this new-found instrument. He was fortunate in obtaining the collaboration of Bitzer, a craftsman-photographer who could be persuaded to experiment, often with miraculous success (see pages 36–38). For example, already in August 1908 in FOR LOVE OF GOLD Griffith demanded a change of camera set-up in the middle of a scene. This was an unheard-of practice. It is remarkable that a man stage-trained as he was should have felt immediately a necessity thus to liberate the motion picture from stage forms and conventions and to compose his film out of brief shots taken at varying distances from the action. But his theatre experience at the same time furnished him with a wealth of plots, as for instance in October 1908, when he drew upon the then familiar play *Ingomar the Barbarian* for one of his pictures. In view of what was to come it must be noted that in November of that year he made his first Civil War subject, THE GUERRILLA, and in the same month for the first time used a social problem as the basis of one of his film plots—THE SONG OF THE SHIRT.

The Griffith-Bitzer collaboration was working well. Early in 1909 they together contrived a strikingly novel effect of light and shade in EDGAR ALLAN POE, and a firelight effect which was widely remarked in the otherwise primitive and stilted A DRUNKARD'S REFORMATION. By June 1909 Griffith was already gaining control of his material and moved to further creative activity. He carried Porter's initial method to a new stage of development in THE LONELY VILLA, in which he employed crosscutting to heighten suspense throughout the parallel scenes where the burglars are breaking in upon the mother and children while the father is rushing home to the rescue. Here he had hit upon a new way of handling a tried device—the last-minute rescue—which was to serve him well for the rest of his career. By March 1911[9] Griffith further developed this disjunctive method of narration in THE LONEDALE OPERATOR, which achieves a much greater degree of breathless excitement and suspense in the scenes where the railwayman-hero is racing his train back to the rescue of the heroine attacked by hold-up men in

Innovations in lighting: Linda Arvidson and Herbert Yost in EDGAR ALLAN POE, *1909.*

Blanche Sweet in THE LONEDALE OPERATOR, *1911.*

Linda Arvidson and Mary Pickford in THE UNCHANGING SEA, *1910.*

the depot. A comparison of the two films—THE LONELY VILLA and THE LONEDALE OPERATOR—shows how far Griffith had progressed in the interim. The camera is used with far more flexibility in the later film and there is a wider variety of set-ups and angles. Perhaps even more noticeable is the brevity and terseness with which each shot is edited. In THE LONELY VILLA many scenes begin quietly with the entrance of the characters into the set; significant action follows this slow-paced start only belatedly. In THE LONEDALE OPERATOR there is no leisurely entrance, the characters are already in midaction when each shot begins and there is no waste footage—no deliberation in getting on with the story when haste and excitement are what is needed. Griffith was relying confidently upon his images to speak eloquently and immediately to the eye and the emotions.

But he was introducing many other innovations and improvements. Gradually (over considerable protest) he was bringing the camera closer and closer to the actors in scenes where it was important to indicate emotional interplay or where small gestures or expressions were of special interest. This had two results: it identified the audience more closely with the action, while it also made the acting much quieter and more intimate. Now very long shots were also introduced, first in RAMONA (May 1910), and afterwards whenever desirable to open up the dramatic horizon, whether for atmosphere or for action. The confines of the stage, so oppressive in earlier films, were being broken, movement in any direction on the screen was employed freely and the motion picture began finally to be a fluid, eloquent and utterly novel form of expression.

Fortunately this creative achievement in a new art form was undertaken so recently that there exists any amount of first-hand evidence as to its effect upon audiences of that time. Mr. Joseph Wood Krutch, for example, vividly recalls that as a boy in Knoxville he and his companions awaited the Biograph pictures of the period with zest because they found them much livelier, more convincing and exciting than other films of the time. Biograph became a name to conjure with; moviegoers were keenly aware of the superiority of its films, and began to grow attached to the players in them. But the man who made the films and the people who acted in them were still anonymous.

Griffith had been instrumental in inducing several competent stage actors to follow his lead and engage in the despised movies—Arthur Johnson, long a leading man in Biograph films, was prominent among them and so was Frank Powell, later to become famous as the inventor of the screen "vamp" and discoverer of Theda Bara when he directed A FOOL THERE WAS (1914). But as Griffith induced Bitzer to take closer and closer shots of the actors, the brilliant Biograph camera became harder and harder on the human face, whether in daylight or in the artificial lighting which was gradually being introduced. Griffith therefore began to gather round him very young people on whose round cheeks time had not yet marked a single line. One of them was a sixteen-year-old veteran of the stage, Mary Pickford, who first played bit parts in WHAT DRINK DID and THE LONELY VILLA and a larger role in THE VIOLIN MAKER OF CREMONA. Three other important newcomers were Blanche Sweet, heroine of many a Biograph picture, Mabel Normand and Mae Marsh. August 1912 brought the two little Gish sisters in AN UNSEEN ENEMY. Robert Harron, at first a studio errand boy, soon graduated to acting. Mary Pickford brought along her young brother Jack. Griffith's method of operation was one well suited to such sensitive children—he customarily rehearsed his scenes until everyone was easy in his role and the cameraman satisfied that all would go well. At no time did he use a scenario. But there was considerable protest when, quite early in his directorial career, he insisted on retaking unsatisfactory scenes and succeeded in gaining permission to do so in THE LONELY VILLA. Bitzer and others were aghast at his extravagance with film.

Yet another innovation was increased length. In May 1911, against considerable opposition, Griffith insisted upon making ENOCH ARDEN in two reels instead of in the customary one. It is true that each reel was released separately, for there was an obstinate belief that audiences could take no more than twelve-minute stories at a time. This belief was to be dispelled, however, by the importation of foreign films of far greater length—innovations in the motion picture as elsewhere have often been accepted more readily when introduced from Europe than when put forward at home. But Griffith has the credit for realizing that the time had come for a larger canvas.

In 1912 Griffith was ready to progress further. He found himself with plenty to say and a new ease in saying it. Social problems had not ceased to interest him and, late in that year, he made one of his finest short pictures, THE MUSKETEERS OF PIG ALLEY. Whether as a study in realism, as an ancestor of the gangster films of later decades or as an exercise in motion-picture composition, this is a remarkable piece. The photography is extraordinary and the whole film predicts what was to come in the modern section of INTOLERANCE. Another noteworthy picture of that year was THE NEW YORK HAT, with Lionel Barrymore as Mary Pickford's champion. This film uses cut-backs, close shots and sharply edited scenes with ease and mastery: close-ups made acting a matter of expression and minute gesture instead of the stereotyped gestures of the popular theatre. The plot for this charming little picture had been submitted by Anita Loos, a sixteen-year-old stage actress in San Diego. At this period, ideas for films were commonly bought from outsiders and members of the company alike. Mary Pickford, Mack Sennett and others contributed many of the plots Griffith used.

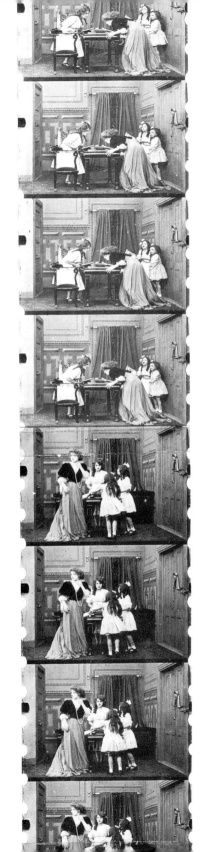

Marion Leonard, Mary Pickford, Adele de Garde in THE LONELY VILLA, *1909.*

Frame enlargements from THE LONELY VILLA, *1909.*

15

below: Henry B. Walthall and Blanche Sweet in JUDITH OF BETHULIA, *1913.*

opposite, left: Lillian Gish at the left in THE MUSKETEERS OF PIG ALLEY, *1912.*

opposite, right: Lillian and Dorothy Gish at the time of their screen debut in AN UNSEEN ENEMY, *1912.*

It is remarkable to what an extent Griffith's films of contemporary life appear in retrospect to excel his period or costume pieces. This is chiefly due to the unconvincingness of the coiffures, costumes, gait, gesture and general air of the actors in period films, whereas the contemporary material by now has the unmistakable veracity of photography by an Atget or a Brady. For this reason it is actually rather difficult to see today why MAN'S GENESIS of June 1912 was an important steppingstone in the whole Griffith progress—yet it unquestionably was one. Described as "a psychological study founded upon the Darwinian Theory of the Evolution of Man," its story of the conflict between brute force and intelligence in a rather sketchy Stone Age provoked discussion and brought a new measure of respect for the motion picture. Griffith felt encouraged to make films with a message. Before long he was to attempt an even more ambitious costume subject of considerable importance—JUDITH OF BETHULIA (1913), the first American four-reel subject. It remains both in his own career and in the memories of those who saw it at the time a real landmark. Lewis Jacobs in *The Rise of the American Film* writes of it: "The unusual form of JUDITH OF BETHULIA, modeled on the four-part pattern of Griffith's earlier PIPPA PASSES, presaged the form of Griffith's future masterpiece, INTOLERANCE. The four movements were in counterpoint not unlike a musical composition; they reacted to each other simultaneously, and the combination produced a cumulative, powerful effect. The individual episodes had a tight internal structure. The imagery was not only lavish in detail but fresh in camera treatment and enhanced by expert cutting." I understand that Mr. Grif-

fith does not like it said that the example of the longer Italian films of the period, like QUO VADIS, had put him on his mettle and encouraged him to fight for the right to make longer films himself, but I believe it to be true. He did not see QUO VADIS, but its very existence made his task easier. JUDITH OF BETHULIA, by reason of its length, its intricate composition, emotional power, ambitiousness and costliness, provided a fitting climax to his long connection with Biograph, though it is also a film which it is difficult wholly to admire today. The company was not prepared to grant him the freedom for expansion which he sought and, late in this year, he severed his connection with it, taking along with him Billy Bitzer and most of the actors and actresses he had gathered about him through the past three years. By now they had emerged from anonymity and were rapidly earning world fame.

Bitzer's recollections of the period are illuminating. "When Mr. Griffith decided to leave Biograph," he writes, "I refused to join with him, although he offered to treble my salary. I didn't think the independent outfit he was going with could possibly stand the gaff of Mr. Griffith's spending of both film and money. Among the inducements Mr. Griffith pictured to me was one in which he said, 'We will bury ourselves in hard work out at the coast for five years, and make the greatest pictures ever made, make a million dollars, and retire, and then you can have all the time you want to fool around with your camera gadgets, etc., and I shall settle down to write.' Now I thought how can he be so sure of that when even now in the pictures we had . . . we never did know whether we had a best-seller until it went out?"

1

2

3

4

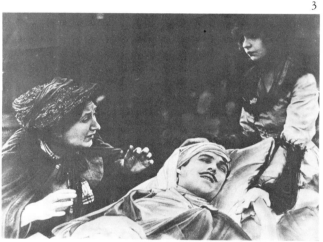

But Griffith was persuasive and so was Mr. Harry Aitken, with whom he had now joined forces under the banner of Mutual films, and Bitzer went along. All was not smooth sailing at first. Griffith rushed THE BATTLE OF THE SEXES through in four days' shooting to provide funds to meet the payroll. "One could sense the money worry from the beginning. . . . They had to hock THE GREAT LEAP, which Christy Cabanne directed, to pay the railroad fares of Mr. Griffith's company to the coast. There wasn't a thing I could see on the horizon of a picture of pictures that would make a million dollars. . . . However, we went along with THE ESCAPE, THE AVENGING CONSCIENCE and HOME SWEET HOME." All three of these films were made at an anxious time. Possibly Griffith gave over the task of making them to other helpers— for they do not (except in flashes and in their ambitious length) really exceed or perhaps even equal the quality of the best Biograph work that preceded them.

Griffith's mind was on the really big picture he was now planning, a story of the Civil War and of the Reconstruction based on Thomas Dixon's novel *The Clansman*. This of course was that "greatest picture ever made" of which Griffith had spoken to Bitzer, which we now know as THE BIRTH OF A NATION.

Bitzer continues: "THE BIRTH OF A NATION changed D. W. Griffith's personality entirely. Where heretofore he was wont to refer in starting on a new picture to 'grinding out another sausage' and go at it lightly, his attitude in beginning on this one was all eagerness. He acted like here we have something worthwhile. . . . Personally I did not share the enthusiasm. I had read the book and figured out that a negro chasing a white girl was just another sausage after all and how would you show it in the South?" However, cameraman and director were perfectly *en rapport;* Bitzer could tell by the look of the back of Griffith's head or a wiggling of his foot whether any given scene had gone well or not. The company was particularly well rehearsed, and everyone flung himself into this new, unbelievably long and ambitious picture. Before it was over the money began to run out, and members of the cast and Bitzer chipped in. Griffith called for new and unheard of effects; he even wanted close-ups of the flying feet of the mounts of the riding Klansmen. Bitzer, down on the ground, did his best as the Klan advanced upon him in a cloud of dust, horses as well as riders half-blinded by flapping sheets. One side of the camera was kicked in, but Bitzer came through. The film was finished, cut, and a special musical score composed for it. It was twelve reels long. Who had ever heard of anything of the sort? Who would show it? Griffith, who was already his own money-raiser, producer and casting director, now had to become his own publicist as well. The few audiences on whom THE CLANSMAN had

1 *The Ride of the Klansmen.*

2 *Henry B. Walthall, as a Confederate officer, is rescued by a boyhood friend, now a Union officer.*

3 *Josephine Crowell, Henry B. Walthall and Lillian Gish.*

4 *Joseph Henabery as Abraham Lincoln.*

This scene of Sherman's March to the Sea in THE BIRTH OF A NATION *is preceded by a close-up of refugees huddled on a hilltop. The camera then moves slowly to the right and irises out to this vast and impressive panorama beyond.*

opposite: *A rehearsal scene: note that the building is not burning.*

left: *The scene as it appears in the film.*

been tried out were swept away by it. A statesman declared it was "like writing history in lightning." The film opened in New York at the Liberty Theatre at $2 a ticket. The most important single film ever made was thus given to the public. The response was overwhelming: people had not realized that they *could* be so moved by what, after all, is only a succession of photographs passed across a screen. All depends, they found, upon what is the order and manner of that passing. THE BIRTH OF A NATION, which had cost about $100,000 to make, grossed $18,000,000 in the next few years. Even more important, it established the motion picture once and for all as the most popular and persuasive of entertainments and compelled the acceptance of the film as art.

The film, however, aroused much opposition and censure.[10] Its subject matter is of a controversial and—to many people—inflammatory nature, though Griffith himself certainly believed he had honestly and impartially told the truth about the South after the Civil War. But he also realized how rich a means of expression he had at his command in this new medium which he himself had so conspicuously helped to develop, and he very naturally insisted on the right of the motion picture to share with literature the privilege of free speech. The protests against THE BIRTH OF A NATION, the moves to censor and muzzle the film threw him into a fighting mood. By his mastery he had unwittingly proved the film to be a most powerful instrument of expression and as a showman he now determined to use it as such.

Intolerance

Before THE BIRTH OF A NATION was released Griffith had almost completed a new picture, THE MOTHER AND THE LAW, a modern story which bleakly revealed the wrongs inflicted by a pious factory owner on his employees and the injustices of which the law may sometimes be capable. Suddenly the new picture seemed to him an insufficiently violent attack on prejudice and cruelty, so that he decided to weave in with his modern story three parallel stories of injustice and prejudice in other ages and so make of the film an epic sermon. The slums of today, sixteenth-century France, ancient Babylon and Calvary itself should speak of the evil which the self-righteous have perpetrated through the centuries. He flung up sets of a size hitherto unimagined, hired players by the hundreds, shot miles of film. Into this gigantic undertaking poured his profits from THE BIRTH OF A NATION. His employees were aghast when he ordered them to construct walls so broad that an army could march round the tops of them, palace halls so vast that the crowds in them were reduced to antlike proportions. Hollywood rang with rumors. The film was two years in the making, yet out of all this footage, extravagance and passion emerged a film of unmistakable greatness and originality called INTOLERANCE.

The Marriage Market, from the Babylonian Story in INTOLERANCE, *1916.*

Battle scene from the Babylonian sequence of INTOLERANCE.

The Feast of Belshazzar from the Babylonian sequence of
INTOLERANCE.

The extravagant Babylonian set designed for INTOLERANCE
in construction on Sunset Boulevard, Hollywood.

The film INTOLERANCE is of extreme importance in the history of the cinema. It is the end and justification of that *Mae Marsh, heroine of the modern story in* INTOLERANCE. whole school of American cinematography based on the terse cutting and disjunctive assembly of lengths of film, which began with THE GREAT TRAIN ROBBERY and culminated in THE BIRTH OF A NATION and in this. All the old and many new technical devices are employed in it—brief, enormous close-ups not only of faces but of hands and of objects; the "eye-opener" focus to introduce vast panoramas; the use of only part of the screen's area for certain shots; camera angles and tracking shots such as are commonly supposed to have been introduced by German producers years later; and rapid crosscutting the like of which was not seen again until POTEMKIN.

The sociological implications of the modern episode seem, perhaps, more pointed now than they did in 1916. They undoubtedly account for the fact that Lenin early in 1919 arranged to have INTOLERANCE toured throughout the U.S.S.R., where it ran almost continuously for ten years. The film was not merely seen there; it was also used as study material for the post-revolutionary school of cinematography, and exercised a profound influence on the work of men like Eisenstein and Pudovkin.[11] It is true that Griffith is largely instinctive in his methods where the Russian directors are deliberate and organized; but it was nevertheless in large measure from his example that they derived their characteristic staccato shots, their measured and accelerated rhythms and their skill in joining pictorial images together with a view to the emotional overtones of each, so that two images in conjunction convey more than the sum of their visible content.

The scale and sumptuousness of JUDITH OF BETHULIA and of INTOLERANCE profoundly affected film-making every-where. At home, they undoubtedly influenced Cecil B. De Mille, whose name later became synonymous with glittering spectacles. In France, the effect of Griffith's work at this period can be traced in the later productions of Abel Gance, and in Germany in those of Fritz Lang. He had conferred both magnitude and complexity as well as expressiveness on the motion pictures and, in Europe and America alike, all the most ambitious films of the 1920s reflected his influence and followed his example.

Though INTOLERANCE has been revived time and again, especially in Europe, unlike THE BIRTH OF A NATION it was not a great popular success. Audiences find it bewildering, exhausting. There is so much in it; there is too much of it; the pace increases so relentlessly; its intense hail of images— many of them only five frames long—cruelly hammers the sensibility; its climax is near hysteria. No question but that the film is chaotic, difficult to take in, or that it has many evident faults. The desire to instruct and to reform obtrudes awkwardly at times. The lyricism of the subtitles accords oddly with the footnotes appended to them. The Biblical sequence is weak, though useful dramatically to point up the modern sequence. The French episode seems to get lost, then reappears surprisingly.

Of the Babylonian and the modern episodes little adverse criticism is permissible, and only admiration remains for the last two reels, when the climax of all four stories approaches and history itself seems to pour like a cataract across the screen. In his direction of the immense crowd scenes, Griffith achieves the impossible, for—despite their profusion and breath-taking scale—the eye is not distracted, it is irresistibly drawn to the one significant detail. The handling of the actors in intimate scenes has hardly been equaled either for depth or for humanity, particularly in the modern sequence and most notably—where a last-minute rescue again serves him well—with Miriam Cooper and Mae Marsh racing to the prison as Robert Harron approaches the gallows. This searching realism, this pulsing life comes not only from Griffith's power to mould his players but, in equal measure, from his editorial skill.

The American film industry by now was passing out of the era of small enterprises and quick individual profits into that of high finance and corporate endeavor.[12] Griffith was not a businessman and he was wholly an individualist. For the future he would often be operating under difficulties. But for the moment the United States was preparing to enter the European war. J. Stuart Blackton's pro-war and anti-German THE BATTLE CRY OF PEACE and Thomas Ince's anti-war and anti-German CIVILIZATION had already indicated the uses to which films might be put and now it was the moment for propaganda for the Allied cause.

Margery Wilson and Eugene Pallette in INTOLERANCE.

Mae Marsh, heroine of modern story in INTOLERANCE.

The climax of the modern story in INTOLERANCE.

Lillian Gish and Noel Coward in HEARTS OF THE WORLD, *1918.*

Griffith in Europe

In the spring of 1917 Griffith received an invitation from the British Government to go to Europe to make a film. This he agreed to do and after a tour of the battlefields began work on HEARTS OF THE WORLD. Part of it was shot in France, part in and around an English village.

HEARTS OF THE WORLD must be judged as a propaganda film and as such it was very effective; but otherwise it seems, on the whole, disappointing. One looks in vain for the passionate momentum of its immediate predecessors. In depicting the plight of women and children in a French village behind the lines it heavily underlines both sentiment and melodrama; the German troops seem almost absurdly "frightful," and the war itself, perhaps of necessity, appears rather sketchy. The film was, however, a personal triumph for Lillian Gish as the distraught heroine, for her sister Dorothy in a comedy role, and for Erich von Stroheim as a German officer. No one who saw the film has ever quite forgotten the scenes in which the heroine wanders dazedly through the landscape bearing her wedding dress carefully in her arms, or the last-minute rescue as she cowers behind an attic door while "the Huns" batter at it with rifle butt and bayonet.

BROKEN BLOSSOMS

Griffith had been absent from Hollywood almost two years when he returned after launching HEARTS OF THE WORLD. His next important film was to be very different. From the large canvas he turned to an intimate photoplay based on "The Chink and the Child," a short story in Thomas Burke's *Limehouse Nights.* Like most of Griffith's films and all of his best ones, it carried a message. The earlier picture had been his contribution to war, but this fairy tale of nonresistance in opposition to violence spoke of international tolerance. The part of the London waif might have been made to measure for Lillian Gish and the choice of Richard Barthelmess as the Chinese boy was fortunate. Work went unusually smoothly and, after the customary period of rehearsal, the film was completed in eighteen days.

When BROKEN BLOSSOMS appeared everyone was overwhelmed, and not only by the discretion and force with which a difficult subject had been handled. Reviewers found it "surprising in its simplicity," and hastened to explain that the photography was misty on purpose, not by accident. The acting seemed a nine days' wonder—no one talked of anything but Lillian's smile, Lillian turning like a tortured animal in a trap, of Barthelmess' convincing restraint. Few pictures have enjoyed greater or more lasting *succès d'estime.*

By 1919 the motion picture was learning fast how to deal freely with ideas and feelings as well as with deeds, and here BROKEN BLOSSOMS, despite its rather theatrical form, played an important part by its scaling down of dramatic action and its intensification of intimate emotion. Possibly Griffith had been influenced by the somber Danish films of the period with their emphasis on atmosphere and on moral and psychological reactions,[13] just as formerly it had been he and Ince who taught the Scandinavians to use an isolated face or gesture as a unit of expression rather than (as on the stage) the actor. In the development of the American film, BROKEN BLOSSOMS marked a distinct stage. Definitely a studio picture, it emphasized a new style of lighting and photography which, though it has been abused, was valuable. In its contrasting periods of calm and of violence it borrowed something from INTOLERANCE, just as the grim finale recalls the death of Mae Marsh in THE BIRTH OF A NATION; but there is a sureness and perhaps a sophistication here which had not formerly been evident. Out of BROKEN BLOSSOMS much was to come. It cannot have been without its influence in Germany; we know that it profoundly affected Louis Delluc and his disciples in France; and, but for it, we might never have had Charles Chaplin's A WOMAN OF PARIS.

A D. W. Griffith Repertory Season opened in May 1919 at the George M. Cohan Theatre in New York with BROKEN BLOSSOMS, followed later by THE FALL OF BABYLON (from INTOLERANCE), "a new peace edition" of HEARTS OF THE

WORLD, and THE MOTHER AND THE LAW (also from INTOL-
ERANCE). During that summer Griffith moved his company
from Hollywood to Mamaroneck, New York, where the old
Flagler estate at Orienta Point was converted into a studio.
Costs had risen sharply and, if Griffith was particularly responsible for this, he was the first to suffer from it. The complex financial operations that had become part of film production were absorbing more and more of his time. He
apparently felt the need to be constantly in or near New
York, which was then as now the financial center and shop
window of the industry.

Griffith, with Mary Pickford, Douglas Fairbanks and
Charles Chaplin, had founded a new joint distributing company, United Artists. THE LOVE FLOWER was the second of
his pictures for them, BROKEN BLOSSOMS being the first;
but in the meantime SCARLET DAYS (1919), THE GREATEST
QUESTION and THE IDOL DANCER (all of relatively minor
importance) had also appeared through other distributors.

Griffith was now faced with an urgent necessity to turn
out a really profitable production. He therefore purchased
for $175,000—far more than the entire cost of THE BIRTH
OF A NATION—the screen rights to a tried and trusted melodrama, *Way Down East*. For this he was much criticized at
first. People considered the play extremely old-fashioned and
said that to adapt it for the screen at that date was "as though
someone were to try to develop 'The Old Oaken Bucket' into
grand opera." Nothing daunted, Griffith set to work in January 1920, and the company began rehearsal while awaiting
snow. All the exteriors were to be real, not studio-contrived.
In March, when a blizzard conveniently came along, the
snowstorm scenes were filmed at Mamaroneck, assistants
hanging on the legs of the cameras to prevent their being
whirled away by the wind, and Miss Gish having to be
thawed out at intervals. The ice scenes were then shot at
White River Junction, Vermont, under peculiarly uncom-
fortable circumstances. Albert Bigelow Paine's *Life and
Lillian Gish* (New York, Macmillan, 1932) quotes Richard
Barthelmess: "Not once, but twenty times a day, for two
weeks, Lillian floated down on a cake of ice, and I made my
way to her, stepping from one cake to another, to rescue
her." The scenes at the brink of the falls were, however,
taken much later in the year at Farmington, Connecticut,
with wooden ice-cakes. The actual waterfall shown for a brief
moment is Niagara. Since scenes of action of this sort are
usually produced today by quite different methods, the facts
seem remarkable, but might hardly be worth recording save
for the effectiveness with which all these scenes taken at
remote times and places were finally assembled.

Richard Barthelmess in BROKEN BLOSSOMS, *1919.*

WAY DOWN EAST proved to be one of the most profitable pictures ever made. The master had once more turned the trick. The public was drawn to see an old favorite in a new guise and found its familiar melodramatic qualities heightened beyond expectation. While sticking faithfully to the bones of the play, Griffith had very rightly adapted it to suit the newer medium—notably at the beginning, by adding material to establish the background of the characters, and at the end to give full rein to the last-minute rescue, developed in purely visual terms and heightened through artful photography and cutting. It was a device which had seldom failed Griffith in the past and stood him in good stead now.

The lapse of time has made it difficult to estimate the qualities of WAY DOWN EAST accurately. Much in it that was fresh and inventive at the time the film was made has since been absorbed into the general repertory of film technique and therefore seems banal. Other devices now outmoded or disused are obtrusive and irritating—the time-lapse fades within single scenes, the low comedy relief, the shots of blossoms and domestic animals interjected for sentiment's sake. The extremely improbable plot creaks loudly, and the musical score, added when the film was re-released in the early days of sound synchronization, seems almost as dated as the Victorian morality. Yet if most of the characterizations are two-dimensional, they are handled with vigor and skill and the study of Anna is entire and convincing. Miss Gish conveys the moods and feelings of the sorely tried heroine more skillfully and with more restraint than she had done in BROKEN BLOSSOMS. Her performance is remarkable for its range, apparent spontaneity and sincerity; it could be contrasted with many contemporary performances to her advantage. Scenes such as the baptism of the dying baby and those in which Anna hears Sanderson confess the mock marriage and David Bartlett declares his love are almost as effective today as they were twenty years ago. The flight through the storm, the ice scenes, and the split-second rescue remain triumphs of direction, camera placement and editing, in which Griffith again attains though hardly surpasses the vitality of THE BIRTH OF A NATION and INTOLERANCE.

The period between INTOLERANCE and WAY DOWN EAST marks the apex of Griffith's success. A figure of international importance, he had played a signal part in founding a huge industry—he had already created a new art form—in which the United States became and remained supreme. Except for Frank Lloyd Wright, no such eminent American as he had arisen in the arts since Whitman. He was to continue active for another decade, though the most fruitful years were past. Already men trained under him were stepping into the limelight, at the same time that newcomers drawn from many walks of life and from Europe as well as from this country

were likewise contributing new ideas, new techniques. Erich von Stroheim, who had been one of Griffith's assistants as well as one of his leading actors, made two films, BLIND HUSBANDS (1919) and FOOLISH WIVES (1921), which attracted wide attention and set a new style. His directorial career—culminating in the superb and somber GREED (1924) —afterwards suffered a great eclipse rendered only the more startling by his re-emergence as an actor in the French film LA GRANDE ILLUSION in 1937. Frank Powell has already been referred to. Mack Sennett, even earlier, had graduated from acting and providing plots for Griffith to the glorious creation of Keystone comedies. Lowell Sherman, villain of WAY DOWN EAST, was to direct—among other films—Mae West's SHE DONE HIM WRONG (1933). Donald Crisp, after BROKEN BLOSSOMS, also became a director of distinction— Buster Keaton's THE NAVIGATOR (1924) and Douglas Fairbanks' DON Q (1925) are perhaps his best-remembered pictures—and today he is again a leading character-actor. It would fill many pages to enumerate the notable actors and actresses who gained their first experience under Griffith and first faced the camera with Bitzer turning. All these fed the industry with new talent. But times and taste alike were changing. From now on Griffith's films were often criticized even by the trade press as "melodramatic." In 1924 James Quirk boldly admonished Griffith in an editorial in *Photoplay:* "You have made yourself an anchorite at Mamaroneck . . . your pictures shape themselves towards a certain brutality because of this austerity . . . your refusal to face the world is making you more and more a sentimentalist. You see passion in terms of cooing doves or the falling of a rose petal . . . your lack of contact with life makes you deficient in humor. In other words, your splendid unsophistication is a menace to you—and to pictures."

Shooting night scenes in the snow at Mamaroneck, New York, for WAY DOWN EAST, *1920.*

31

Lillian and Dorothy Gish in ORPHANS OF THE STORM, *1922.*

Made in Germany in 1924, ISN'T LIFE WONDERFUL *was the first film to dramatize the tragedies of defeat and hunger in Central Europe.*

ORPHANS OF THE STORM

But in ORPHANS OF THE STORM (1921), and again despite an old-fashioned story, Griffith's ability to individualize characters, handle crowds and sustain suspense stood him in good stead. The film was liked by the public. Lillian and Dorothy Gish again scored a triumph, while Monte Blue and Joseph Schildkraut won innumerable admirers. Even today, despite such minor irritations as the silly subtitles and the awkward (if traditional) staring and groping of the blind girl, this film can grip one's attention. That cannot be said of his next picture, THE WHITE ROSE (1923), yet in 1922 it was Griffith who had once and for all set the pattern for the murder-mystery film in ONE EXCITING NIGHT. And his next two pictures were still notable for the emotion they had the power to conjure up, for the splendor of their photography and for their scope and boldness. AMERICA (1924) was not another BIRTH OF A NATION, but it was a film which few other directors at that time would have attempted. ISN'T LIFE WONDERFUL, also 1924, is a little masterpiece. Here we have the curious spectacle of seeing the man who had made the anti-German and violent HEARTS OF THE WORLD now produce a sensitive and often touching pro-German picture which most forcibly conjures up the tragedy of defeat and hunger in Central Europe. ISN'T LIFE WONDERFUL lacks the shock-value of the more powerful scenes in Pabst's THE JOYLESS STREET, made the following year and treating a similar subject, but it bears comparison with it, though the American film—much of it shot in Germany—was the late product of an old master while THE JOYLESS STREET was the second film of a new one. Among all Griffith's later pictures this one wears best.

It was to be his last independent production for some time to come; if one were to write of him only in terms of the adulation he and his career as a whole command, a review of his extraordinary achievements might best end here. From this time on he was to work usually under conditions ill-suited to his temperament and experience, while business and financial problems of increasing complexity beset him. At the age of fifty, when he had already directed hundreds of films which include the most profoundly original films ever made, he was placed in competition with much younger men who inherited ready-made the technique he had perfected through arduous years. Obviously they were far better able than he to adopt new methods, to adapt themselves to changing tastes and to represent the postwar age.

There is nothing surprising in the fact that Mr. Griffith, during this period on contract to Famous Players-Lasky, grew less than himself. In our own time many of the more gifted film-makers chafe continually under studio conditions and long to work independently—as Griffith originally did. In 1925 he had been his own master for too long to submit easily or fruitfully to control. But the burden of motion picture financing and distribution forced him of necessity into the service of a large corporation. The results were painful and costly to him, and the films were not excellent. It would be only just to recall that, under far less hampering conditions, artists in other media—Monet and Tennyson, for example—have at comparable stages in their careers also entered upon a period of decline.

Griffith and the Talkies

Nevertheless, with his next independent production, ABRAHAM LINCOLN (1930), it looked as though the master were back in his stride. The industry had undergone a severe shaking up with the advent of sound in 1927, and the time was propitious for the "come-back" of an old-timer. This sound film with Walter Huston in the title role was hailed as "a Griffith achievement," and when the votes were taken early in 1931 for the best director of 1930 it was Griffith who won the distinction. For a man who had been making films continuously since 1907 this seems an extraordinary feat. Griffith himself contends, however, that ABRAHAM LINCOLN would have been a much better picture had he not been compelled to make it, as he says, "all dry history with no thread of romance." But in December 1931 his talking picture THE STRUGGLE saw the light and was much less favorably received. *The Film Daily,* for instance, wrote: "This is poor entertainment; it is an old-fashioned domestic drama with little box-office appeal." Perhaps this estimate was correct. The theme and spirit of the film were substantially those of Griffith's THE DRUNKARD'S REFORMATION of 1908, though alcoholism had become a topic of intense interest since Prohibition. In truth THE STRUGGLE seems pedestrian and inept today, an impression rendered worse by the poor sound recording,—but not in comparison with the average film of 1930. And there are some remarkable moments in it.

Were we to regard THE STRUGGLE as Mr. Griffith's swan song, this brief account of his career would seem to end on a minor air. Henceforth this great pioneer steps into the limelight only occasionally and then, alas, too often in connection with lawsuits, receiverships, and the like. It seems a very long time since the Biograph days. The children who tripped to fortune up the steps of 11 East 14th Street are all of them middle-aged or dead, and "Billy" Bitzer has fallen on evil days. It is true that the sun shines on perennially youthful Lillian Gish, her sister Dorothy and Mary Pickford, and that Lionel Barrymore's name remains one to conjure with. It is true that Mr. Griffith himself can match for looks and sheer force of personality any man twenty years his junior—he gives an extraordinary air of enjoying life while being somewhat detached from it. He even professes to think it rather amusing, if pleasant, that anyone should bother about his old films. But ours is a very different world from the one he triumphed in; a simple story of right overcoming wrong at the last moment no longer serves as a scenario, and no one will ever create the art of the motion picture again. It is enough that Griffith *did* create it but—humanly— his story at this later stage has some bitterness in it.

Lionel Barrymore in THE CHIEF'S BLANKET, *1912.*

When Griffith set out to film the Civil War for THE BIRTH OF A NATION, he did it alone and in secrecy. Only his closest staff members knew the magnitude of the production he had in mind, and they were constantly astonished as the vision grew before their eyes. AMERICA, which involved the filming of the Revolutionary War, was made in the full glare of publicity and with the help of historians and historical societies. Griffith welcomed the cooperation of such bodies as the Daughters of the American Revolution because of the promotional value, and through their efforts AMERICA was seen as an ideal vehicle to teach school children about their heritage and the winning of freedom from oppression. As a not the sort of man who forgets. After mutual greetings, Van Dyke asks Griffith if he will take over the direction, and Griffith consents "just for fun." And so part of the memorable scene of mass action in SAN FRANCISCO where principals and extras climb the hill, was made not by Van Dyke but by "old Colonel Jacob Griffith's son," who had set out from Louisville so many years earlier to seek fame and fortune. He had won both, though not in the direction he then anticipated, and had seen both recede. But the `men who make films today know who it was that taught them the basis of their craft. The American public, which for forty-five years has so keenly enjoyed and supported the motion picture, has been somewhat reluctant to allow it the status of an art. Now, gradually, they too are recognizing that in Griffith they have one of the greatest and most original artists of our time.

Iris Barry

Sheridan's ride in ABRAHAM LINCOLN, *1930. United Artists.*

1 It consisted of Jim White, a stage-struck blacksmith, of Ned Ridgely, steamboat comedian and small-town barnstormer, of Griffith, and occasionally of landlords who took out in histrionic experience what they had been unable to collect in rent.

2 He left the 100-acre property "Safe Guard" in Worcester County, Maryland, to his daughter Nancy Beauchamp; a Negro girl to his granddaughter Nancy Owen Bowles; the property "Abergildie" in Somerset County, Maryland, to his son Merlin, and the rest of his estate (save for one Negro woman who was to obtain her freedom) to his sons Jefferson, Salathiel William and Daniel Weatherby, who were to be apprenticed as soon as they were old enough.

3 Now West Virginia.

4 In his later years "Roaring Jake" enjoyed immense local fame for the Shakespearean readings he gave at church socials. People would drive in from miles around to hear him.

5 These and many other details are drawn from the incomplete manuscript of an autobiography *D. W. Griffith and the Wolf* which Mr. Griffith permitted us to consult.

6 August 2, 1909, Griffith signed a second contract at $50 a week plus 1/10 of 1 per cent for each lineal foot of positive film sold, the firm to pay him the difference should this commission plus salary in any week be less than $100.

7 August 1, 1910, Griffith signed a third contract at $75 a week plus a commission of 1/8 of 1 per cent for each lineal foot of positive film leased or sold, the firm to make up the difference should this commission plus salary in any week be less than $200.

8 November 11, 1911, Griffith signed a fourth contract at $75 a week plus a commission of 1 3/4 mills for each lineal foot of positive film leased or sold, the firm to make up the difference should this commission plus salary in any one week be less than $200.

9 From January 1910 on, the company wintered in California. Mrs. Griffith's book gives many picturesque details of trips on location to Cuddebackville and of adventures in the real Wild West which well illustrate the tenor and spirit of those fourteen-hour days. According to Bitzer, from the time he entered Biograph until he attended the Boston opening of THE BIRTH OF A NATION in April 1915, Griffith himself took not even one day's vacation. He and his company were a hard-working and highly cooperative bunch, not well paid by present-day standards but buoyed up by the success of their work and the feeling, surely, of being in the thick of something both vigorous and novel. The actors contributed stories and helped with one another's costumes and make-up, the cameraman was not above handling props, the director cut his own film, anybody around the studio would enact a part or do a laborer's job if necessary.

10 See Terry Ramsaye: *A Million and One Nights,* New York, 1926, reprinted 1964, pages 641-644.

11 In September 1936 Leonid Trauberg, codirector with G. Kozintsev of such noted Russian pictures as NEW BABYLON and THE YORTH OF MAXIM, wrote to Mr. Griffith from Moscow asking for details of his biography to be incorporated in an encyclopedic *Lives of Illustrious Men:*

"I take the liberty to count myself one of your pupils, though I think there are hardly such people in our art which do not count themselfs so.

. . . You certainly know what an important effect your pictures have had on Soviet cinema directors and actors. We have seen your pictures in 1923-4—except INTOLERANCE in 1919—i.e. in that time when we all—Eisenstein, Pudovkin, Ermler, Vassilieffs and we two—had just begun our work as directors. Under the influence of your pictures as BROKEN BLOSSOMS, DREAM STREET, WAY DOWN EAST, ORPHANS OF THE STORM and others our style has been created. Especially lately, during the last 3-4 years we have examined your work with more intense interest, chiefly because we find in it that power, humanity and realism which we also try—in our own way—to attain in our pictures."

12 In May 1915 Griffith together with Thomas H. Ince and Mack Sennett became the star-directors of a new producing organization, Triangle Film Corporation, which introduced Douglas Fairbanks, Sir Herbert Beerbohm Tree, Constance Collier, Raymond Hitchcock, William S. Hart and numerous other stage luminaries to the screen.

The subsequent stages of Mr. Griffith's business career are so involved as to require a separate essay. During his career Griffith is said to have spent about $20,000,000 on some 400 pictures which earned about $60,000,000.

13 Mr. Griffith corrects this suggestion: he says that he had never seen any Danish films, although they were rather widely shown.

Griffith in 1916. A publicity picture inscribed "To D. W. my former boss and unsuspecting teacher" in 1936 by the ace-director, W. S. Van Dyke.

Griffith's Cameraman,
Billy Bitzer: An Interview by Beaumont Newhall

When Griffith joined Biograph he was fortunate to find in the studio G. W. Bitzer, who had been with the company since 1896, first as electrician, but soon as a jack-of-all-trades —cameraman, property man, scenic designer and director. The two at once became companions, and for sixteen years Bitzer almost single-handedly realized on film the action that Griffith directed. They worked together so closely that it is virtually impossible to separate their technical contributions. Bitzer, when interviewed in 1940, vividly recalled this remarkable teamwork. His mechanical ingenuity enabled him to realize some of Griffith's revolutionary ideas. But Bitzer remembered with humor that some of the devices Griffith used so effectively were stumbled upon by accident.

The Mutograph camera used by Biograph in the early 1900's was a clumsy instrument. One of its great drawbacks was that film could not be re-rolled for a double exposure. This meant that the company could not make trick films, which were then very popular. Perhaps this purely mechanical deficiency of equipment made Griffith's ideas particularly attractive to the Biograph financiers, for it offered them a way to meet competition through novelty. Bitzer recollects that this camera was used for a long time in the Biograph studio. It could be driven by hand or by a motor. Raw film, without the familiar marginal perforations of today, was put into the camera; during the shooting two holes per frame were punched out, and the celluloid disks fell through the bottom of the camera case onto the ground in a steady stream. Bitzer could easily duplicate a camera set-up by putting his tripod over the little pile of celluloid disks. Static electricity, generated by the friction feed of the film, caused trouble; to overcome it the interior of the camera was heated with a shielded bicycle lamp which burned alcohol. But in cold weather, when static was most severe, the heat brought further trouble—condensation on the lens. The film scratched easily, and these scratches showed up so prominently in sky areas that it was necessary to exclude as much sky as possible in the composition of the shots. Yet out of this crude equipment came some of the finest photography seen on the screen, and the catalog of innovations is staggering.

Many of these innovations began as accidents which Bitzer turned into practical techniques. A less imaginative and courageous director than Griffith would have hesitated to recognize their esthetic and dramatic value. This is not the place to discuss priority; the importance of these devices lies in their functional, almost automatic, origin and in their brilliant exploitation.

Slow film which is "unbacked"—which has not been coated with an opaque light-absorbing substance on its reverse side—is prone to exaggerate highlights in a most dis-

Constance Talmadge in INTOLERANCE.

tressing way. Points of light seem to spread and to eat up adjacent darker details. This *halation* can be partially prevented by shading the lens with a tubular hood. Photographing one day by electric light in his basement, Bitzer improvised such a lens hood from an old glue pot. The results were fine, so fine that he took his home-made gadget on location. But when the film was processed the corners of each frame appeared rounded off in darkness. Bitzer had forgotten an elementary optical fact—that the iris diaphragm in the lens which controls the amount of light falling on the film also affects the focus. Like the human eye, the iris of the camera eye is wide open in dim light and constricted in bright light. Objects near and far are sharp when the camera iris is small. Inadvertently, by closing the camera iris to the small diameter demanded by brilliant sunlight, Bitzer had brought the end of his lens hood into focus. When Griffith saw the projected film he was far from disappointed. "He got very excited," Bitzer told the writer, "and asked me how I'd gotten the new effect. I said that I'd been working on it quietly for the last six months!"

The logical step was to contrive a lens hood which could be adjusted to give more pronounced effects. A large iris diaphragm from a still camera was added to the hood. To adjust it more easily a handle was fastened to the flimsy setting. This led to another accident. During the shooting the weight of the handle closed the iris gradually; the dark corners of the frame grew until the image was entirely blotted out. Again technical failure resulted in recognition by Griffith of a new device, the fade-out. "This was just what we needed," pointed out Bitzer. "The climax of all these films was the kiss. We couldn't linger over the embrace, for then

yokels in the audience would make cat-calls. We couldn't cut abruptly—that would be crude. The fade-out gave a really dignified touch; we didn't have a five-cent movie any more."

But the vignette mask was not always satisfactory; it cut out part of the scene. To subdue the corners of the frame and direct the eye towards the principal action the gauze mask was developed—simply a couple of layers of black chiffon fastened over the hood with a rubber band. Holes were burned in the gauze with the end of a cigarette where the image detail should be distinct. Further experiments were made with iris diaphragms made of translucent celluloid, with graduated filters and with "barn doors"—a box with four sliding members which could be pushed in at will to change the rectangular proportions of the frame. The front of Bitzer's camera became notorious, and rival cameramen would bribe actors to give them detailed reports on his latest gadget.

Bitzer claims that THE BIRTH OF A NATION was shot with just one camera. It seems incredible, but the program credit bears him out. "It was a $300 Pathé machine," he reminisced, "with a 3.5 two-inch lens interchangeable with a wide-angle lens—that is, you had to screw one out and screw the other into its place. None of your turrets like they have today, where the cameraman presses a button and the six-inch lens pops into place! It was a light camera, and it was easy to pick it up and come forward for a close-up, back for a long shot, around for a side angle. But there were times when I wished that Mr. Griffith wouldn't depend on me so much, especially in battle scenes. After all, a fellow doesn't want to spend all his time in dusty California adobe trenches. The fireworks man shooting smoke bombs over the camera—most of them exploding outside the camera range and D. W. shouting 'Lower, lower, can't you shoot those damn bombs lower?' 'We'll hit the cameraman if we do,' answered the fireworks brigade, and bang!, one of them whizzed past my ear. The next one may have gone between my legs for all I knew. But the bombs were coming into the camera field so it was O.K.

opposite: *Bitzer at the camera, Griffith directing Henry Walthall, in a posed publicity picture at about the time of* DEATH'S MARATHON, *1913.*

"All we had was orthochromatic film. Perhaps this old stock with its limited range of tones really helped the BIRTH OF A NATION photography—it sort of dated the period not only in the battle scenes but in the historical events like Lee's surrender."

This realistic quality has often been remarked. Individual shots have been compared to Brady's Civil War photographs. The similarity is not accidental, for Bitzer, bribing a librarian with a box of chocolates, got hold of some photographic copies of the famous Civil War series for Griffith's use. Besides the quality of the slow orthochromatic film, light played a very important part in the picture. Daylight was used exclusively in THE BIRTH OF A NATION, except in the night shots lighted by flares. Throughout his career Bitzer has used daring lighting, even to the extreme of allowing light to fall directly on the lens. Reflectors were used to soften shadows, bringing out their detail, but always in a subdued way so that their presence is unnoticed in the film. These reflectors were "soft"—they were of cloth, not casting the harsh light of a polished metal, tin-foil or other "hard" reflector. Bitzer likes to tell about how he stumbled on back, or reverse, lighting. During a lunch hour on Fort Lee location he playfully turned his lens on Mary Pickford and Owen Moore as they were eating sandwiches, and ground out a few feet of film without their knowledge. The two were between the camera and the sun, but Bitzer went ahead—after all, the sequence was intended only as a joke, to liven up the projection room audience. Enough light happened to be reflected into their faces to hold the detail, and when it was screened Griffith was more than amused—since it indicated a new approach to lighting.

Fate had not dealt kindly with Billy Bitzer when we interviewed him at the request of Iris Barry eight years before his death. He was no longer a working cinematographer and his contribution to our film heritage was then hardly known. We shall ever remember his pride of craftsmanship and his affection for "D.W." His pioneer achievements rank among the most significant and remarkable in film history.

Beaumont Newhall

Shooting the "ride to the rescue" in the modern story of IN-TOLERANCE. *Bitzer at the camera, Griffith at extreme right.*

An Annotated List of the Films of D. W. Griffith
by Eileen Bowser

While preparing the following list of Griffith's films, I have consulted the standard works on Griffith, in particular Linda Arvidson Griffith's *When the Movies Were Young,* Robert Edgar Long's *David Wark Griffith,* Seymour Stern's *An Index to the Creative Work of David Wark Griffith* (through HEARTS OF THE WORLD), and unpublished program notes by William K. Everson, as well as contemporary accounts in *The Moving Picture World* and the daily press. However, I have drawn most of my information from The D. W. Griffith Collection of business and personal papers in the possession of The Museum of Modern Art. All letters quoted or referred to are in the Collection. I have screened all of the films discussed with the exception of THE BATTLE OF THE SEXES and LADY OF THE PAVEMENTS.

Exploration:
the films made for the Biograph Company

The films made at the beginning of Griffith's career for the Biograph Company represent his greatest contributions to the art of the film. They are not as ambitious or as famous as his masterworks, THE BIRTH OF A NATION and INTOLERANCE, but in them Griffith made all the discoveries for which he is remembered today and which made his later films possible. An amazing number of them survive, though many remain in negative or paper print form only. They still await serious study by the film historian. To realize the importance of Griffith's achievements in his Biograph period, it is necessary only to view films made by anyone else in the world during the years 1908-13.

The following list was compiled by Katherine Stone from original Biograph record books and with the assistance of G. W. Bitzer. In a few cases it varies from that published by Seymour Stern in the invaluable "An Index to the Creative Work of David Wark Griffith, Part I," *British Film Index Series,* 2, April 1944. The titles followed by a question mark are those which Miss Stone concluded were probable Griffith films although definite proof was lacking. The titles marked with an asterisk are not credited by Stern, while those in parentheses are credited by Stern but not by Katherine Stone. The date given after the title is the release date. (See also pages 9–10 for Iris Barry's comments on some of the Biograph films.)

1908
The Adventures of Dollie, July 14
The Fight for Freedom,* July 17
The Black Viper,* July 21
The Tavern-Keeper's Daughter,* July 24
The Redman and the Child, July 28
Deceived Slumming Party,* July 31
The Bandit's Waterloo, August 4
A Calamitous Elopement, August 7
The Greaser's Gauntlet, August 11
The Man and the Woman, August 14
The Fatal Hour, August 18
For Love of Gold, August 21
Balked at the Altar, August 25
For a Wife's Honor, August 28
Betrayed by a Handprint, September 1
Monday Morning in a Coney Island
  Police Court,* September 4
The Girl and the Outlaw, September 8
Behind the Scenes, September 11
The Red Girl, September 15
The Heart of O Yama, September 18
Where the Breakers Roar, September 22
A Smoked Husband, September 25
The Stolen Jewels, September 29
The Devil, October 2
The Zulu's Heart, October 6

Father Gets in the Game, October 9
The Barbarian—Ingomar, October 13
The Vaquero's Vow, October 16
The Planter's Wife, October 20
The Romance of a Jewess, October 23
The Call of the Wild, October 27
Concealing a Burglar, October 30
After Many Years, November 3
The Pirate's Gold, November 6
The Taming of the Shrew, November 10
The Guerrilla, November 13
The Song of the Shirt, November 17
The Ingrate, November 20
A Woman's Way, November 24
The Clubman and the Tramp, November 27
The Valet's Wife, December 1
Money Mad, December 4
The Feud and the Turkey, December 8
The Reckoning, December 11
The Test of Friendship, December 15
An Awful Moment, December 18
The Christmas Burglars, December 22
Mr. Jones at the Ball, December 25
The Helping Hand, December 29

1909
One Touch of Nature, January 1
The Maniac Cook, January 4
Mrs. Jones Entertains, January 7
The Honor of Thieves, January 11
Love Finds a Way, January 11
A Rural Elopement, January 14
The Sacrifice, January 14
The Criminal Hypnotist, January 18
Those Boys!, January 18
Mr. Jones Has a Card Party, January 21
The Fascinating Mrs. Francis, January 21
The Welcome Burglar, January 25
Those Awful Hats, January 25
The Cord of Life, January 28
The Girls and Daddy, February 1
The Brahma Diamond, February 4
A Wreath in Time, February 8
Edgar Allan Poe, February 8
Tragic Love, February 11
The Curtain Pole, February 15
His Ward's Love, February 15
The Hindoo Dagger, February 18
The Joneses Have Amateur Theatricals,
    February 18
The Politician's Love Story, February 22
The Golden Louis, February 22
At the Altar, February 25
His Wife's Mother, March 1
The Prussian Spy, March 1
A Fool's Revenge, March 4
The Roué's Heart, March 8

The Wooden Leg, March 8
The Salvation Army Lass, March 11
The Lure of the Gown, March 15
I Did It, Mamma, March 15
The Voice of the Violin, March 18
The Deception, March 22
And a Little Child Shall Lead Them,
    March 22
A Burglar's Mistake, March 25
The Medicine Bottle, March 29
Jones and His New Neighbors, March 29
A Drunkard's Reformation, April 1
The Road to the Heart, April 5
Trying to Get Arrested, April 5
A Rude Hostess, April 8
Schneider's Anti-Noise Crusade, April 8
The Winning Coat, April 12
A Sound Sleeper, April 12
Confidence, April 15
Lady Helen's Escapade, April 19
A Troublesome Satchel, April 19
The Drive for a Life, April 22
Lucky Jim, April 26
Twin Brothers, April 26
'Tis an Ill Wind that Blows No Good,
    April 29
The Eavesdropper, May 3
The Suicide Club, May 3
The Note in the Shoe, May 6
One Busy Hour, May 6
Jones and the Lady Book Agent, May 10
The French Duel, May 10
A Baby's Shoe, May 13
The Jilt, May 17
Resurrection, May 20
Eloping with Aunty, May 24
Two Memories, May 24
The Cricket on the Hearth, May 27
Eradicating Aunty, May 31
His Duty, May 31
What Drink Did, June 3
The Violin Maker of Cremona, June 7
The Lonely Villa, June 10
A New Trick, June 10
The Son's Return, June 14
Her·First Biscuits, June 17
The Faded Lilies, June 17
Was Justice Served?, June 21
The Peachbasket Hat, June 24
The Mexican Sweethearts, June 24
The Way of Man, June 28
The Necklace, July 1
The Message, July 5
The Country Doctor, July 8
The Cardinal's Conspiracy, July 12
The Friend of the Family, July 15
Tender Hearts, July 15

The Renunciation, July 19
Jealousy and the Man, July 22
Sweet and Twenty, July 22
A Convict's Sacrifice, July 26
The Slave, July 29
A Strange Meeting, August 2
The Mended Lute, August 5
Jones' Burglar, August 9
They Would Elope, August 9
The Better Way, August 12
With Her Card, August 16
His Wife's Visitor, August 19
Mrs. Jones' Lover, or "I Want My Hat,"
    August 19
The Indian Runner's Romance, August 23
Oh, Uncle, August 26
The Seventh Day, August 26
The Mills of the Gods, August 30
Pranks,* August 30
The Little Darling, September 2
The Sealed Room, September 2
"1776," or The Hessian Renegades,
    September 6
Comata, the Sioux, September 9
The Children's Friend, September 13
Getting Even, September 13
The Broken Locket, September 16
In Old Kentucky, September 20
A Fair Exchange, September 23
Leather Stocking, September 27
The Awakening, September 30
Wanted, a Child, September 30
Pippa Passes, or The Song of Conscience,
    October 4
Fools of Fate, October 7
The Little Teacher, October 11
A Change of Heart, October 14
His Lost Love, October 18
The Expiation, October 21
In the Watches of the Night, October 25
Lines of White on a Sullen Sea, October 28
The Gibson Goddess, November 1
What's Your Hurry?, November 1
Nursing a Viper, November 4
The Restoration, November 8
The Light That Came, November 11
Two Women and a Man, November 15
A Midnight Adventure, November 18
Sweet Revenge, November 18
The Open Gate, November 22
The Mountaineer's Honor, November 25
In the Window Recess, November 29
The Trick That Failed, November 29
The Death Disc, December 2
Through the Breakers, December 6
The Redman's View, December 9
A Corner in Wheat, December 13

A Beast at Bay, May 27
An Outcast among Outcasts, May 30
Home Folks, June 6
A Temporary Truce, June 10
Lena and the Geese, June 17
The Spirit Awakened, June 20
The School Teacher and the Waif, June 27
Man's Lust for Gold, July 1
An Indian Summer,* July 8
Man's Genesis, July 11
Heaven Avenges,* July 18
The Sands of Dee, July 22
Black Sheep (?), July 29
The Narrow Road, August 1
A Child's Remorse, August 8
The Inner Circle, August 12
A Change of Spirit, August 22
Swords and Hearts, August 28
The Stuff Heroes Are Made Of,*
    September 4
The Old Confectioner's Mistake,*
    September 7
The Squaw's Love, September 14
Dan, the Dandy,* September 18
The Revenue Man and the Girl,
    September 25
Her Awakening, September 28
The Making of a Man, October 5
Italian Blood, October 9
The Unveiling, October 16
The Adventures of Billy, October 19
The Long Road, October 26
Love in the Hills, October 30
The Battle, November 6
The Trail of Books, November 9
Through Darkened Vales, November 16
The Miser's Heart, November 20
Sunshine Through the Dark, November 27
A Woman Scorned, November 30
The Failure, December 7
Saved From Himself, December 11
As In a Looking Glass, December 18
A Terrible Discovery, December 21
The Voice of the Child, December 28

1912
The Baby and the Stork,* January 1
A Tale of the Wilderness, January 8
The Eternal Mother, January 11
The Old Bookkeeper, January 18
For His Son, January 22
A Blot in (sic) the 'Scutcheon, January 29
The Transformation of Mike, February 1
A Sister's Love,* February 8
Billy's Stratagem, February 12
The Mender of Nets, February 15
Under Burning Skies, February 22

The Sunbeam, February 26
A Siren of Impulse, March 4
A String of Pearls, March 7
Iola's Promise, March 14
The Root of Evil, March 18
The Goddess of Sagebrush Gulch, March 25
The Girl and Her Trust, March 28
The Punishment, April 4
Fate's Interception, April 8
The Female of the Species, April 15
Just Like a Woman, April 18
One Is Business, the Other Crime, April 25
The Lesser Evil, April 29
The Old Actor, May 6
A Lodging for the Night, May 9
His Lesson, May 16
When Kings Were the Law, May 20
A Pueblo Legend, August 29
(In the North Woods, September 2)
An Unseen Enemy, September 9
(Blind Love, September 12)
Two Daughters of Eve, September 19
Friends, September 23
So Near, Yet So Far, September 30
A Feud in the Kentucky Hills, October 3
(The Chief's Blanket, October 10)
In the Aisles of the Wild, October 14
The One She Loved, October 21
The Painted Lady, October 24
The Musketeers of Pig Alley, October 31
Heredity, November 4
The Massacre, November 7[3]
Gold and Glitter,* November 11
My Baby,* November 14
The Informer, November 21
Brutality, December 2
The New York Hat, December 5
My Hero,* December 12
The Burglar's Dilemma,* December 16
A Cry For Help,* December 23
The God Within, December 26

1913
Three Friends, January 2
The Telephone Girl and the Lady,
    January 6[4]
Pirate Gold (?),* January 13
An Adventure in the Autumn Woods,*
    January 16
The Tender-Hearted Boy,* January 23
A Misappropriated Turkey (?),* January 27
Brothers,* February 3
Oil and Water, February 6
Drink's Lure (?),* February 17
A Chance Deception,* February 24
Love in an Apartment Hotel,* February 27

Broken Ways, March 8
A Girl's Stratagem (?),* March 10
The Unwelcome Guest,* March 15
Near to Earth,* March 20
Fate, March 22
A Welcome Intruder (?),* March 24
The Sheriff's Baby, March 29
The Hero of Little Italy (?),* April 3
The Perfidy of Mary,* April 5
The Little Tease, April 12
A Misunderstood Boy, April 19
The Left-Handed Man (?),* April 21
The Lady and the Mouse, April 26
If We Only Knew (?),* May 1
The Wanderer,* May 3
The House of Darkness, May 10
The Stolen Loaf (?),* May 15
The Yaqui Cur, May 17
Olaf—an Atom (?),* May 19
Just Gold, May 24
His Mother's Son, May 31
The Ranch Hero's Revenge (?),* June 2
A Timely Interception,* June 7
Death's Marathon, June 14
The Switch Tower (?),* June 16
The Mothering Heart, June 21
In Diplomatic Circles (?),* June 26
Her Mother's Oath,* June 28
The Sorrowful Shore,* July 5
The Enemy's Baby (?),* July 10
The Mistake, July 12
Doing the Round-Up (?),* July 19
The Coming of Angelo,* July 26
The Reformers, or The Lost Art of Minding
    One's Business, August 9
An Indian's Loyalty (?),* August 16
Two Men of the Desert, August 23

*The following films, made by Griffith in the
summer of 1913, were not released by Biograph until after he had left the company.*

1914
The Battle at Elderbush Gulch, March 28,
    2 reels
Judith of Bethulia, March 8, 4 reels

Expansion:
the films made for the Mutual Film Corporation

In October 1913 Griffith joined Reliance-Majestic, which distributed through the Mutual Film Corporation. He was hired as head of production and took with him the best of the Biograph Company's talent. There he produced THE GANGSTERS OF NEW YORK, DOPE, RUY BLAS, FROU FROU, SAPHO (*sic*), MOTHS, THE GREAT LEAP, THE MOUNTAIN RAT, THE FLOOR ABOVE, and others. He personally directed the films listed below. Although he remained titular production chief until the formation of Triangle in July 1915, his working days were taken up with the production of THE BIRTH OF A NATION, the supervision of its road shows, and the shooting of THE MOTHER AND THE LAW, and he had no time for direct supervision of other films from July 1914 to the end of his Mutual association.

The following films, all written and directed by Griffith, were photographed by G. W. Bitzer, who had signed a three-year personal contract with Griffith on October 9, 1913.

THE BATTLE OF THE SEXES
Opened at Weber's Theatre, New York, April 12, 1914. Based on *The Single Standard* by Daniel Carson Goodman. 5 reels.
Cast:
Jane Andrews *Lillian Gish*
Frank Andrews *Owen Moore*
Mrs. Frank Andrews *Mary Alden*
The Siren *Fay Tincher*
and *Donald Crisp, Robert Harron*

Made as a "quickie" before Griffith left for California, THE BATTLE OF THE SEXES served the purpose of raising money for the new company. Even the title was good box office. The story was the old one of the straying husband, the home-wrecker and the forgiving wife. Lillian Gish played the part of a daughter who was moved by her mother's sufferings to the point of committing murder. Griffith remade the film in 1928 (page 81). A brief excerpt is all that is known to remain of this first version.

THE ESCAPE
Opened at the Cort Theatre, New York, June 1, 1914. Based on the play by Paul Armstrong. 7 reels.
Cast:
May Joyce *Blanche Sweet*
Jennie Joyce *Mae Marsh*
Larry Joyce *Robert Harron*
McGee *Donald Crisp*
Dr. Von Eiden *Owen Moore*
The Father *F. A. Turner*
The Senator *Ralph Lewis*

Based on a sensational play of the day, THE ESCAPE was about eugenics, poverty and crime, and may be grouped with Griffith's sociological studies. Part of it was shot in the streets of New York, but it was completed on the West Coast, where the movie industry was flourishing and where the Griffith company was to be based for the next five years. THE ESCAPE was held up in release until after HOME, SWEET HOME. No prints of THE ESCAPE are known to exist today.

HOME, SWEET HOME

Opened at the Strand, New York, May 17, 1914. 6 reels.
Cast:
I Prologue and Epilogue
John Howard Payne *Henry B. Walthall*
His Mother *Josephine Crowell*
His Sweetheart *Lillian Gish*
Her Sister *Dorothy Gish*
The Worldly Woman *Fay Tincher*
II
Apple Pie Mary *Mae Marsh*
Her Father *Spottiswoode Aiken*[5]
The Easterner *Robert Harron*
His Fiancé *Miriam Cooper*
III
The Mother *Mary Alden*
Her Sons *Donald Crisp, James Kirkwood, Jack Pickford*
The Sheriff *Fred Burns*
IV
The Husband *Courtenay Foote*
The Wife *Blanche Sweet*
The Tempter *Owen Moore*
The Musician *Edward Dillon*

HOME, SWEET HOME is made up of several stories with a common theme: the sentiment of the title song as reflected in the life of its composer, John Howard Payne, and in three other episodes. In this it forecasts INTOLERANCE, although here the stories are not intercut. All the stories concern people who are moved by thoughts of home, yet there is variety. The Prologue and Part III end in tragedy, whereas the other stories end happily. One is rural in setting, while another takes place in the city. Part II is set on the California coast with an exciting ride-to-the-rescue along the sands, probably the only Griffith last-minute rescue which arrived too late. For a finale Griffith created an allegory (another parallel to INTOLERANCE), in which John Howard Payne, held back by Lust and Greed, struggles to get out of the pit to his sweetheart, Lillian Gish, who has been transformed into an angel suspended by wires.

The development of parallel editing and the elaboration of framing devices are of special interest as Griffith moves toward the greater complexities of INTOLERANCE. It is not quite accurate to say, as Stern does in his *Index,* that this is the first time the mounted moving camera was used. This kind of shot was a popular gimmick before the turn of the

Donald Crisp in THE ESCAPE, *1914.*

opposite: *Lillian Gish, Fay Tincher, Owen Moore in* THE BATTLE OF THE SEXES, *1914.*

century, with cameras mounted on trains and trolleys, and Griffith himself had already used it in A GIRL AND HER TRUST. All the techniques which Griffith was popularly credited with inventing have their forerunners. But in most cases he was the one who originated a story-telling or dramatic use for them and incorporated them into the body of film narrative technique.

THE AVENGING CONSCIENCE

Previewed in Pasadena, California, July 16, 1914, opened at the Strand, New York, August 2, 1914. Suggested by Edgar Allan Poe's "The Telltale Heart" and "Annabel Lee." 6 reels.
Cast:
The Nephew *Henry B. Walthall*
His Sweetheart *Blanche Sweet*
The Uncle *Spottiswoode Aiken*
The Italian *George Seigmann*
The Detective *Ralph Lewis*
The Maid *Mae Marsh*

THE AVENGING CONSCIENCE is an ambitious study in psychology and atmosphere. Henry Walthall's uncle wants to prevent his marriage to Blanche Sweet, and Walthall, reading

Poe's works, broods over the thought of murdering him. In visions he sees his dead uncle, Moses with the Ten Commandments and Christ on the Cross. THE AVENGING CONSCIENCE was more elaborately produced than any previous film, with double exposures, framing devices that move around the screen, editing for comparison and contrast and, for symbolic purposes, some extreme close-up photography of a spider and a fly. Grisly details alternate with lovely outdoor scenes—among the latter a real Pasadena society garden fete. Probably only Griffith's prestige at this time could have so far overcome California society's prejudice against "those picture people."

THE AVENGING CONSCIENCE takes the spectator inside the mind of the protagonist, and at the end we find the murder has taken place only there. In its concern with psychological matters, THE AVENGING CONSCIENCE is a precursor to THE CABINET OF DR. CALIGARI and other German films which were later to rival Griffith's films in the public mind. When Griffith began to feel the pinch of competition from German films in the early 1920s, he was a little annoyed. He felt with some justice that his ideas were being used against him— ideas that he had himself long since discarded.

Blanche Sweet and Henry Walthall in an allegorical scene from THE AVENGING CONSCIENCE, *1914.*

Edward Dillon in HOME, SWEET HOME, *1914.*

The first masterwork: THE BIRTH OF A NATION

THE BIRTH OF A NATION

Opened as THE CLANSMAN in Los Angeles, February 8, 1915, and as THE BIRTH OF A NATION at the Liberty Theatre, New York, March 3, 1915. 12 reels.

Directed by D. W. Griffith; screenplay by Griffith, assisted by Frank Woods, based on the novel and the play, *The Clansman*, with additional material from *The Leopard's Spots*, all by Thomas Dixon; photographed by G. W. Bitzer, assisted by Karl Brown; music arranged by Joseph Carl Breil and Griffith.

Cast:

Elsie, Stoneman's daughter *Lillian Gish*
Flora Cameron, the pet sister *Mae Marsh*
Col. Ben Cameron *Henry Walthall*
Margaret Cameron, elder sister *Miriam Cooper*
Lydia, Stoneman's mulatto housekeeper *Mary Alden*
Hon. Austin Stoneman, Leader of the House *Ralph Lewis*
Silas Lynch, mulatto Lieut. Governor *George Seigmann*
Gus, a renegade Negro *Walter Long*
Tod, Stoneman's younger son *Robert Harron*
Jeff, the blacksmith *Wallace Reid*
Abraham Lincoln *Joseph Henabery*
Phil, Stoneman's elder son *Elmer Clifton*
Mrs. Cameron *Josephine Crowell*
Dr. Cameron *Spottiswoode Aiken*
Wade Cameron, second son *André Beringer*
Duke Cameron, youngest son *Maxfield Stanley*
Mammy, the faithful servant *Jennie Lee*
Gen. U. S. Grant *Donald Crisp*
Gen. Robert E. Lee *Howard Gaye*
Sen. Charles Sumner *Sam de Grasse*
John Wilkes Booth *Raoul Walsh*
and *Elmo Lincoln, Olga Grey, Eugene Pallette, Bessie Love, Jennie Lee, William de Vaull, Tom Wilson*
On the original screen credits for the film only the names of D. W. Griffith and Thomas Dixon appeared, but subsequently the other names listed above were given in the credits and in the programs.

The following notes supplement Miss Barry's comments on pages 19–22.

Griffith's supreme achievements, THE BIRTH OF A NATION and INTOLERANCE, are so important in the history of cinema that each deserves a volume to itself. A body of literature already exists but the exhaustive critical-historical analysis has yet to be made. Eleven enormous scrapbooks bulging with newspaper clippings hold the material which Griffith himself collected in the first year of THE BIRTH OF A NATION's run. And Griffith's treatment of race relations in THE BIRTH OF A NATION has been discussed in countless articles and has been the subject of at least two academic theses to date.

Playscripts in the Griffith Collection of the Film Library indicate that Griffith probably worked from the stage version of *The Clansman*, a popular road show of the day. The old Kinemacolor Company, whose former studios Griffith was occupying, had tried to film *The Clansman*, using the cast of the touring company and filming throughout the Southern states as the company traveled. After spending some $25,000, however, the company abandoned this somewhat unrealistic project. Frank Woods, who wrote the continuity, came to work for Griffith and, according to Linda Arvidson's account in *When the Movies Were Young*, suggested the subject to him.

A letter from Harry Aitken to Griffith dated April 15, 1914 reveals that agreement had already been reached about the film being produced as a Mutual release:
"I think your next feature should be an Elderbrush [*sic*] Gulch film . . . [referring to the earlier film made for Biograph, the proposed sequel spoken of here was not made] . . . and then we will get after "The Clansman."

Though Aitken was one of the chief backers of THE BIRTH OF A NATION and reaped its income for many years, he must have been staggered as the project expanded into the most ambitious production the film industry had envisioned. The financing of it soon outgrew the Mutual-Majestic resources, and an independent company, the Epoch Producing Corporation, was incorporated on February 8, 1915, to finance and distribute it with Harry Aitken as president and Griffith its vice-president.

G. W. Bitzer has left written record of the locations where the film's sequences were shot: the fir tree scenes at Big Bear Mountain; the cotton field in Calexico; the battle scenes at what later became the Universal lot; and all other interior and exterior scenes at the Reliance-Majestic studio and the adjoining lot at the corner of Sunset and Hollywood Boulevards.

There is reason to doubt Terry Ramsaye's story in *A Million and One Nights* that Thomas Dixon suggested the new title THE BIRTH OF A NATION after a showing at the Rose Gardens in New York on February 20, 1915. Trade papers were by then using the new name. But Ramsaye may have been wrong only about the date. The film did open in California as THE CLANSMAN, and was often called by this name on the West Coast in later years.

THE BIRTH OF A NATION is probably the only film of its period which can still move an audience to the heights of emotion. This may account for endless controversies about its message, for other films, such as Lubin's COON TOWN SUFFRAGETTES and Turner's IN SLAVERY DAYS, which are much more blatantly racist, have long since been forgotten. It is not easy to be objective about THE BIRTH OF A NATION today. It must be kept in mind that the film was a Southerner's honest effort to portray events still very close to the experience of the community in which he grew up. Griffith had the native attitudes of the Southern tradition. At the same time he was a nineteenth-century romantic. But above all he was a dramatist: he was a genius at portraying emotion by means of the language of the screen. Examples from THE BIRTH OF A NATION that have been particularly admired include: the mother and children huddled on a hilltop, the camera panning and the iris opening to full screen to reveal an extreme long shot of soldiers marching in the valley below (inspired by Griffith's spying a little group of extras eating lunch oblivious to the battle scenes beyond them); Henry Walthall offering his canteen to a wounded enemy soldier, or a few moments later, charging wounded, carrying the flag; the soldier guarding the hospital door who gazes with longing at Lillian Gish and sighs; the shot of an arm coming out of a doorway, the unseen mother gently drawing inside her son returned home; and the famous ride of the Ku Klux Klan, gathering momentum with increasingly frequent short shots intercut with other streams of action and building to an extraordinary climax.

The problem that confronts archivists and scholars who hope to find complete original versions of films is insurmountable where Griffith's major work is concerned. This is true even though The Museum of Modern Art in 1939 acquired the surviving negative that Griffith himself owned.[6] As is well known, he did not work from shooting scripts until forced to by employers when he worked under contract. He personally supervised the editing and, whenever possible, even the printing in the laboratory. When THE BIRTH OF A NATION opened, he spent all his time at the Liberty Theatre, cutting shears in hand, editing and improving according to audience reaction. Not content with this procedure in New York, where in agreement with Mayor Mitchell and the License Commissioner he eliminated some of the more inflammatory shots, he followed the film to its openings in Boston, Chicago and Los Angeles, adjusting the prints in each city. Since this was his practice when road-showing INTOLERANCE and other important work, Griffith's films were not likely to be the same at the end of a run as they had been on opening night.

Charles Chaplin, Mary Pickford, D. W. Griffith, Douglas Fairbanks in 1919, at the time of their founding of United Artists.

Interlude:
the films made for the Triangle Film Corporation

In July 1915 Harry Aitken, the entrepreneur who had lured Griffith from Biograph to the Mutual fold and the chief backer of THE BIRTH OF A NATION, talked Thomas Ince, Mack Sennett, and D. W. Griffith into forming a single company, the Triangle. Each of the three men was already a highly successful producer and had his own large studio in operation and each continued to supervise his team of directors while Aitken handled distribution and exploitation. In the first few months of the new project, Griffith produced a number of films for Triangle (under the trademark "Fine Arts"), but he personally directed none of them. He was soon so involved with INTOLERANCE, which grew each day into a more and more ambitious production, that he had little or no time for attention to the Triangle films. As soon as INTOLERANCE opened he went off to give it the same careful attention he had devoted to THE BIRTH OF A NATION. Consequently many of the films that were later credited to him could not have received his personal supervision. Of course Aitken was anxious to use the great Griffith name for publicity and Griffith was still careless with its use, but when he came to the end of his Triangle association and finally separated from Aitken he began to disavow all Triangle films. On October 1, 1916, Griffith was interviewed by Louella Parsons in Chicago, where he had been supervising the opening days of INTOLERANCE, and said:

"I haven't seen a Triangle picture in four months. I have never produced a Fine Arts production, and the words 'supervised by David W. Griffith' were put on the screen without my knowledge. My time has been spent making *Intolerance* which has occupied all my waking hours."

This was a slight exaggeration, but from this time on, though he continued to produce films which he did not direct, he was jealous of his name and would not let it be used.

The directors, actors and everyone else at the Fine Arts studio had been trained by Griffith and did their best to follow the Griffith style. But his supervision never resembled that of Ince, who gave shot by shot scripts to his directors with instructions not to deviate in any detail. The directors under Griffith at Triangle were John Emerson, William Christy Cabanne, Paul Powell, S. A. and C. M. Franklin, Chester Withey, Lloyd Ingraham, Allan Dwan and Edward Dillon.

There is evidence that from time to time Griffith took an active hand in the production of some of the films. In his 1933 radio series, for instance, he reminisced about difficulties with the energetic Douglas Fairbanks on the set of THE LAMB, the film that was his first contribution to the Fine Arts-Triangle program. Fairbanks, who was among Aitken's new acquisitions from the New York stage, returned to Triangle's eastern studios to make his third film, HIS PICTURE IN THE PAPERS, and Griffith had little to do with his films after the first one or two.

Another early film in which Griffith participated, according to circumstantial contemporary accounts, was THE FLYING TORPEDO. This was begun in July, 1915, but not released until 1916. THE FLYING TORPEDO is a science fiction forecast of 1921, in which the west coast United States is invaded by the "yellow peril," and it features a torpedo controlled by wireless. Another Griffith-supervised film, OLD HEIDELBERG, released in the fall of 1915, had a pacifist theme, but by the time THE FLYING TORPEDO appeared preparedness was the word of the hour.

The trade periodical *The Moving Picture World* gives an eyewitness account of Griffith taking over the direction of part of HOODOO ANN (1916), in which Mae Marsh played the orphan asylum heroine who is pursued by bad luck but who finds a happy home at last, a favorite story of the movies in the teens. This was Mae Marsh's Triangle debut. Griffith believed strongly in her ability though other Triangle executives did not, and he quarreled over her with Aitken, who said she had no drawing power. When in the fall of 1916 Mae Marsh was hired away to be one of the top stars of Samuel Goldwyn's new company, Griffith was understandably bitter. He telegraphed Aitken: "I would suggest that you attend to managing the Triangle which is conceded to be the worst managed business in Film History. . . ."

In addition to casting and assigning film projects to directors Griffith wrote original scenarios for a number of Triangle films. For some reason he chose not to take credit for them and wrote under the pseudonym "Granville Warwick." A number of these films were listed as "adapted from Granville Warwick's novel," though no such novels ever were published. The Triangle films credited to that prolific author are as follows:

1915
The Lamb, directed by William Christy Cabanne
The Lily and the Rose, directed by Paul Powell

1916
Let Katy Do It, directed by S. A. and C. M. Franklin
The Missing Links, directed by Lloyd Ingraham
The Wood Nymph, directed by Paul Powell
Daphne and the Pirate, directed by William Christy Cabanne
Hoodoo Ann, directed by Lloyd Ingraham
Diane of the Follies, directed by William Christy Cabanne

The second masterwork: INTOLERANCE

INTOLERANCE[7]

Previewed at Riverside, California, August 6, 1916, opened at the Liberty Theatre, New York, September 5, 1916. 14 reels.
Directed by D. W. Griffith; photographed by G. W. Bitzer, assisted by Karl Brown; music arranged by Joseph Carl Breil and Griffith.
Cast:
The Woman Who Rocks the Cradle *Lillian Gish*

The Modern Story
The Girl *Mae Marsh*
Her Father *Fred Turner*
The Boy *Robert Harron*
Jenkins *Sam de Grasse*
Mary T. Jenkins *Vera Lewis*
Uplifters *Mary Alden, Pearl Elmore, Lucille Brown, Luray Huntley, Mrs. Arthur Mackley*
The Friendless One *Miriam Cooper*
Musketeer of the Slums *Walter Long*
The Policeman *Tom Wilson*
The Governor *Ralph Lewis*
The Judge *Lloyd Ingraham*
Father Farley *Rev. A. W. McClure*
Friendly Neighbor *Max Davidson*
Striker *Monte Blue*
Debutante *Marguerite Marsh*
Owner of Car *Tod Browning*
Chief Detective *Edward Dillon*
Jenkins' secretary *Clyde Hopkins*
The Warden *William Brown*
Wife of the Neighbor *Alberta Lee*

The Judean Story
The Nazarene *Howard Gaye*
Mary the Mother *Lillian Langdon*
Mary Magdalene *Olga Grey*
Pharisees *Gunther von Ritzau, Erich Von Stroheim*
Bride of Cana *Bessie Love*
Bridegroom *George Walsh*

Medieval French Story
Brown Eyes *Margery Wilson*
Prosper Latour *Eugene Pallette*
Her Father *Spottiswoode Aiken*
Her Mother *Ruth Handforth*
The Mercenary *A. D. Sears*
Charles IX *Frank Bennett*
Duc d'Anjou *Maxfield Stanley*
Catherine de Medici *Josephine Crowell*
Marguerite de Valois *Constance Talmadge*[8]
Henry of Navarre *W. E. Lawrence*
Admiral Coligny *Joseph Henabery*

Babylonian Story
The Mountain Girl *Constance Talmadge*
The Rhapsode *Elmer Clifton*
Belshazzar *Alfred Paget*
Princess Beloved *Seena Owen*
King Nabonidas *Carl Stockdale*
High Priest of Bel *Tully Marshall*
Cyrus, the Persian *George Seigmann*
The Mighty Man of Valor *Elmo Lincoln*
Judge *George Fawcett*[9]
Old Woman *Kate Bruce*
Solo Dancer *Ruth St. Denis*
Slave *Loyola O'Connor*
Charioteer *James Curley*
Babylonian Dandy *Howard Scott*
Girls of the Marriage Market *Alma Rubens, Ruth Darling, Margaret Mooney*
Favorites of the Harem *Mildred Harris, Pauline Starke, Winifred Westover*

Many other later famous performers played bit parts and served as extras. Colleen Moore, commonly attributed a bit part, could hardly have been in it, however, for she met Griffith for the first time when he was in Chicago to arrange for the opening of INTOLERANCE. *He signed her to a contract and she went to Los Angeles, but she never played a role in a Griffith-directed film after all.*

The following notes supplement Miss Barry's comments on pages 23–27.

A separate company, formed to finance and distribute INTOLERANCE, was incorporated in December 1915 with the name of the Wark Producing Corporation. Because the handful of investors in Epoch got rich, many were eager to invest in the new company. Griffith was the largest single investor, but there were nearly fifty others, including Harry and Roy Aitken, Lillian Gish and Mae Marsh. Wark went bankrupt in 1921. Griffith "lent" the company money during 1922–23 to help pay off its debts, enabling him to retain all the rights to INTOLERANCE.

In addition to INTOLERANCE, Wark distributed the two films that were later cut from it, THE MOTHER AND THE LAW and THE FALL OF BABYLON. Griffith had thought of this way to recoup money as soon as he realized that INTOLERANCE was not a box office success. In August 1917 he cabled instructions from London to "Preserve all INTOLERANCE discards perhaps may use in separate stories later." More money had to be poured into Wark to pay for the exploitation of the two films, and little if any profit remained.

The Los Angeles fire department ordered immediate dismantling of the giant INTOLERANCE sets in 1916, no doubt because they were not built in accordance with the local building code. Incredibly, these sets had been built without any architectural plans—they just grew from day to day as Griffith had new ideas and told his carpenters what he wanted. Griffith managed to delay the job of dismantling them until the fall of 1917, but they were so solidly built that parts of them survived on back lots of Hollywood many years later.

The problem of finding a complete archival print of IN-TOLERANCE is compounded by the fact that late in 1918 the original negative was cut to make the negatives for two separate films, THE FALL OF BABYLON and THE MOTHER AND THE LAW. In December 1919, when a print of INTOL-ERANCE was needed to fulfill a contract in Brazil, the studio reported that there were no good copies on hand and that none could be printed because the negative no longer existed in its original form. The negatives for THE FALL OF BABYLON and THE MOTHER AND THE LAW were needed to fill other orders. In order to avoid a threatened lawsuit a patched-up used print of INTOLERANCE was supplied to Brazil. Griffith later tried to restore the INTOLERANCE negative, but it was never as long as the original. It has been estimated from the running time that INTOLERANCE was about 13,500 or 13,700 feet at the time it opened, though Lillian Gish remembers seeing an earlier four-hour version. Prints ordered to fill foreign contracts during the 1920s averaged fewer than twelve reels, while prints supplied to London in 1922 only amounted to ten-and-one-half reels. The remaining negatives and prints were acquired by the Film Library in 1938. Using a combination of materials, the Film Library now has a preservation copy, not to be projected but preserved as an archive copy, measuring 11,811 feet, including an introductory title attached to it. We cannot know if in the climax the incredibly swift cutting and rhythmic pace is just as it was in the 1916 version, but it remains a powerful experience.

There never existed a written script for the film; it was all in Griffith's head. He tried to reconstruct good prints for the 1926 and 1933 revivals, but they were also short versions. His mental picture of the film probably changed in seventeen years—just as he had changed. Griffith never stopped trying to improve his films. As Paul Valéry said: "A work of art is never completed, but merely abandoned," and instead of completing his films, Griffith eventually abandoned them.

The hazards of filming on such a large scale were recalled by Griffith in his 1933 radio series. He described the pre-dawn hours of the day scheduled for filming the Fall of Babylon sequence, with some 15,000 people and 250 chariots on call. The sun alone was to be the source of light.[10] The weather bureau had been checked, but in addition a half-dozen men were stationed sixty miles apart to report by telephone on a fog bank that was progressing in the direction of the location. On its fate depended 15,000 salary checks and 15,000 box lunches and a thousand other details. Before daylight Griffith gave the order to proceed to location, and the scene was filmed just before the fog arrived.

D. W. Griffith in France, 1917.

The results of fame:
HEARTS OF THE WORLD
and the films made for Artcraft Pictures

By now Griffith was at the height of his fame, and it is interesting to speculate on the effect the acclaim that greeted him everywhere may have had on his personality. Brought up in poverty and without adequate education, Griffith had aspirations to be a great writer, in particular a great playwright . Now he was hailed as the Shakespeare of the screen and he walked with the great of his time, the wealthy and the socially prominent. Although he knew he had poured his heart into THE BIRTH OF A NATION and INTOLERANCE, he must have been a bit bewildered to have achieved such success in the medium he had originally despised. His was an intuitive genius, and fame made him self-conscious. His deliberate striving for artistic excellence or for popularity

Lillian Gish and Robert Harron in HEARTS OF THE WORLD, *1918.*

in his later films led him at times to descend into mannerism. The financial failure of INTOLERANCE made him painfully aware of the need to cater more to popular taste, yet he was never sure of what popular taste was. No amount of success quite gave him full confidence in his powers, and failure, when it did arrive, was what he had been half-expecting all the time. His written and spoken words at times became pompous, at times cynical. As the failures grew more frequent toward the end of his career, the cynicism predominated.

HEARTS OF THE WORLD

Opened at the 44th Street Theatre, New York, April 4, 1918. 12 reels.

Directed by D. W. Griffith; scenario by M. Gaston de Tolignac, translated into English by Capt. Victor Marier (both pseudonyms for D. W. Griffith); photographed by G. W. Bitzer; technical supervision by Erich Von Stroheim; music arranged by Carli Elinor and Griffith.

Cast:
The Grandfather *Adolphe Lestina*
The Mother *Josephine Crowell*
The Girl, Marie Stephenson *Lillian Gish*
The Boy, Douglas Gordon Hamilton *Robert Harron*
The Father of the Boy *Jack Cosgrave*
The Mother of the Boy *Kate Bruce*
The Littlest Brother *Ben Alexander*
The Boy's Other Brothers *M. Emmons, F. Marion*
The Little Disturber *Dorothy Gish*
Monsieur Cuckoo *Robert Anderson*
The Village Carpenter *George Fawcett*
Von Strohm *George Siegmann*
The Innkeeper *Fay Holderness*
A Deaf and Blind Musician *L. Lowy*
A Poilu *Eugene Pouyet*
A French Peasant Girl *Anna Mae Walthall*
A Refugee *Mlle. Yvette Duvoisin of the Comédie Française, Paris Paris*
A French Major *Herbert Sutch*
A Poilu *Alphonse Dufort*
A Poilu *Jean Dumercier*
Stretcher Bearers *Gaston Riviere, Jules Lemontier*
A Poilu *Georges Loyer*
A German Sergeant *George Nicholls*
A Refugee Mother *Mrs. Mary Gish*
Woman with Daughter *Mrs. Harron*
Wounded Girl *Mary Harron*
Refugee *Jessie Harron*
Boy with Barrel *Johnny Harron*
Dancer *Mary Hay*
Not credited on the original programs: Erich Von Stroheim as a Hun in several scenes, and Noel Coward as the Man with the Wheelbarrow and as a Villager in the Streets.

On March 17, 1917, Griffith sailed for London to attend the opening of INTOLERANCE and to discuss a British offer to make a propaganda film for the war effort. On the same date he announced his Triangle severance and the signing of a contract with Artcraft, Adolph Zukor's company that produced for Famous Players-Lasky (or Paramount, as it was to become known).

Zukor, whose firm had already swallowed most of Triangle's directors and stars, put up some of the money for HEARTS OF THE WORLD in exchange for eventual distribution rights as well as a guarantee of future Griffith films.[11] Thus began a long relationship between Griffith and Zukor. Although the latter did not function as Griffith's boss, his suggestions had the force of coming from the man most interested in the financial success of the film. Nevertheless, Griffith retained ownership of HEARTS OF THE WORLD, raising money for it on his own reputation. After it was completed, he supervised its presentation, distribution and the sale of rights in conjunction with Zukor. The financing of HEARTS was even more complicated than Griffith's previous big films; nevertheless Griffith handled it personally.

HEARTS OF THE WORLD has long been neglected as a major Griffith film. A shortage of good prints has probably contributed more to its disappearance than its immediate propagandistic purpose and a nearly complete version now made should help to restore admiration for it. Griffith had several motives in making it. He was enormously impressed by the welcome he received in England (he became a confirmed Anglophile and a lifelong friend of Lord Beaverbrook), and he needed money badly to recover from the debts of the Wark Corporation. But when he had toured the battlefields, slogged through muddy trenches and observed the suffering of soldiers and civilians alike, he was genuinely determined to recreate the scene for the benefit of Americans.

Publicity men created myths about the production of HEARTS OF THE WORLD, claiming that it consisted largely of on-the-spot recording of events. For the most part, Griffith recreated scenes which he witnessed or learned about first hand—Lillian Gish trying to guide her confused grandfather to safety as the village is bombarded; the orphaned children burying their mother's body in the cellar. The only Americans who joined Griffith for filming in France and England were the two Gish girls and their mother, Robert Harron, George Fawcett, George Seigmann, Ben Alexander and his mother, and Bitzer with several assistants; even Von Stroheim was not hired until the company returned to California. The scenes in which other members of the Griffith company appeared must have been shot on the West Coast, and, though Griffith and Bitzer toured the front lines photographing action scenes, Griffith added stock footage later. When the war began a Captain Kleinschmidt, who had been lecturing here on his explorations and travels, filmed the German armies on the battlefield and showed them in New York. After the United States entered the war on the side of the Allies, Captain Kleinschmidt (an Austrian) was arrested as a spy, and Griffith paid him $16,000 for his films. An exchange of telegrams between Griffith in California and his New York office reveals Griffith's use of the Kleinschmidt battle footage in HEARTS OF THE WORLD. The question of how much of HEARTS OF THE WORLD was shot by Griffith on the battlefields of France may never be solved. The audited accounts report that the Los Angeles charges against negative costs were more than twice those incurred abroad.

The original purpose of the film was to convince Americans to enter the war, but before Griffith could begin work, America had entered. The S.S. Baltic, on which Bitzer, Robert Harron and Dorothy Gish sailed for England on May 28, 1917, carried as another passenger General Pershing. America was unprepared, however, and it was almost a year before her armies were well enough organized to help turn the tide. The propaganda aim became our transformation into an angry, fighting people. It was a short war for America, and HEARTS OF THE WORLD had not been released long before the Armistice was in sight. The picture made a lot of money quickly—its profit by the end of 1918 was more than $500,000—before being drastically cut and altered to fit the peace. Zukor wanted a shorter film for Artcraft distribution, and while Griffith fought him for the major showings under his own supervision, wiring his New York office ". . . if picture is big enough twelve reels is short enough . . .," he consented to a shorter version for general distribution. The peacetime alterations naturally included eliminating scenes that would arouse hatred of the Germans. The film which had begun in twelve reels ended up in eight. Fortunately for archivists, complete shot lists exist for the original and subsequent versions, made up for the use of Griffith's cutters[12] when the heavy demand for prints prevented Griffith from supervising all of them.

"Viewed as drama," Griffith said, "the war is disappointing." Wisely, he chose to portray the awesome holocaust in terms of a few individuals in a small village that changes hands as the fortunes of war sweep over it. The organization of his film was discursive in the manner of the rambling nineteenth-century novels on which he grew up. In the abbreviated versions it was incredibly jumpy, but in the restored film there is time to elaborate the elements of the story. Griffith discarded forever the brilliant pyrotechnics of INTOLERANCE, settling down to an assured style in which technical means do not often call attention to themselves. The spectator is moved by, though scarcely aware of, the beautiful slow camera movement that discloses Lillian Gish to the eyes of Robert Harron as he falls in love with her. The next few years might be called the "Gish period" in Griffith's career, with Lillian Gish playing the lead in one film after another, continually growing in stature as an actress. But Dorothy Gish all but steals this film away from her. Without any really funny material to work with except her own elastic face and jaunty movements, she used her role to launch a magnificent career as star of a long series of comedies.

Griffith used long explanatory titles to avoid interrupting the flow of action with dialogue titles, the more popular method with other film-makers. As time went on he was much criticized for his titles even by critics who admired his films. Titling was a problem never completely solved in the silent period, and certainly not by Griffith.

As for HEARTS OF THE WORLD's effectiveness as propaganda, the young Kenneth MacGowan, writing in *The New Republic* of July 1918, while deploring the lack of restraint in bloody scenes of violence, said:

"Here we have an art of pure emotion which can go beneath thought, beneath belief, beneath ideals, down to the brute fact of emotional psychology, and make a man or a woman who has hated war, all war, even this war, feel the surge of group emotion, group loyalty and group hate."

Griffith made several contributions to the war effort along with other Hollywood notables. He made personal appearances to sell war bonds, and produced a one-reel film for the Liberty Loan Appeal starring Lillian Gish, and with Carol Dempster and Kate Bruce. The film was completed in September 1918. In it, Lillian's mother urges her to buy bonds but she prefers to buy clothes until she has a dream of German atrocities which stirs her to patriotism when she awakes. No prints are known to exist today.

Long before HEARTS OF THE WORLD was ready for release Griffith set in motion a number of programmers for his Artcraft contract, and in December 1917 leased his old Fine Arts studio from Triangle. His first such Artcraft project, THE HUN WITHIN, was one with which his name was not formally associated. He wrote the script (with assistance from S. E. V. Taylor) under his old pseudonym Granville Warwick, and the film was directed by Chet Withey. Griffith probably made use in it of footage left over from HEARTS OF THE WORLD (which was to supply scenes for several of his next pictures) and he cast it with Dorothy Gish, George Fawcett, Erich Von Stroheim and other members of the stock company. He invested his own money in THE HUN WITHIN, and once again a separate organization, the F-4 Company, was formed to finance it. The completed film was later sold to Famous Players-Lasky at a profit of over $25,000.

When Griffith returned to Los Angeles from the opening of HEARTS OF THE WORLD he began directing his own Artcraft films. While he retained ownership of HEARTS, the other films he made went to Paramount under the separation agreement at the end of the contract with Zukor. Because of the deterioration of the original negatives that were placed in Paramount's vaults, only two of these films are known to exist today.

At the same time that Griffith directed the Artcraft films he contracted with Artcraft to produce a series of comedies starring Dorothy Gish (wearing the same black wig she had worn in HEARTS OF THE WORLD) and work was begun on the series after the star completed a sensational personal-appearance tour with HEARTS OF THE WORLD. Griffith spent more money on these comedies than he did on the films he was directing, but he declined to have his name attached to the series. The directors included Elmer Clifton, Chet Withey, F. Richard Jones, and Dorothy Gish's sister Lillian, who directed REMODELING HER HUSBAND all by herself at the half-completed Mamaroneck studios while Griffith was off getting lost in southern waters (see page 61-62). The co-star in the later films of the series was James Rennie, who became Dorothy Gish's husband. Zukor advanced production costs in exchange for distribution rights, and the comedies provided a steady income for Griffith.

The Dorothy Gish Artcraft Series:

1918
Battling Jane

1919
The Hope Chest
Boots
Peppy Polly
I'll Get Him Yet
Nugget Nell
Out of Luck (Nobody Home)
Turning the Tables

1920
Mary Ellen Comes to Town
Remodeling Her Husband
Little Miss Rebellion
Flying Pat
Ole Swimmin' Hole
(production #13, no record of release)

1921
The Ghost in the Garret
Oh, Jo

1922
The Country Flapper
(released by Producers Security Corporation)

The following Artcraft films were all directed by D. W. Griffith and photographed by G. W. Bitzer:

THE GREAT LOVE

Opened at the Strand, New York, August 11, 1918. 7 reels.

Scenario by Capt. Victor Marier (D. W. Griffith and S. E. V. Taylor).

Cast:

Jim Young, of Youngstown, Pa. *Robert Harron*
Sir Roger Brighton *Henry B. Walthall*
Jessie Lovewell *Gloria Hope*
Susie Broadplains *Lillian Gish*
John Broadplains *Maxfield Stanley*
Rev. Josephus Broadplains *George Fawcett*
Mademoiselle Corintee *Rosemary Theby*
Mr. Seymour of Brazil, formerly of Berlin *George Seigmann*

and *Queen Alexandra, Lady Diana Manners, Miss Elizabeth Asquith, and the Princess of Monaco as themselves.*

Billed as "D. W. Griffith's second great European photoplay," THE GREAT LOVE dealt with the adventures of a young American who is fired up by the German atrocities in Belgium and enlists in the British army before America's entry into the war. In London he meets and falls in love with an innocent young Australian girl who, as an heiress, is pursued by an unscrupulous fortune hunter. The youthful love affair is interrupted by the war, and "the machinations of German adventurers masquerading as radicals." The film made use of scenes Griffith had taken in England showing real society debutantes who are transformed from social butterflies into war workers in hospitals and factories. Griffith himself made an appearance à la Hitchcock as a passerby in the streets. No prints of THE GREAT LOVE are known to exist today.

D. W. Griffith, left, prepares to shoot a scene for THE GREAT LOVE, *1918, with Mrs. Buller,* Lady Diana Manners, Miss Elizabeth Asquith *and the Duchess of Beaufort representing English society. The sequence was made in England in the summer of 1917, when Griffith was working on* HEARTS OF THE WORLD.

Opened at the Strand, New York, January 26, 1919.
6 reels.
Scenario by Capt. Victor Marier (D. W. Griffith).
Cast:
Old Lady Smiles *Lydia Yeamans Titus*
John L. Logan, Jr. *Robert Harron*
Mrs. Logan *Kate Bruce*
John L. Logan, Sr. *George Fawcett*
Jennie Timberlake *Lillian Gish*
Her Father *George Nicholls*
Vinegar Watkins *Adolphe Lestina*
Judas *Bertram Grassby*
The Negro Farmhand *Porter Strong*

Griffith avoided the war in his next film. He had begun
to call his Artcraft productions a "short story series," and
explained he wanted to return to the simple narratives of his
Biograph days. The story he wrote for A ROMANCE OF HAPPY
VALLEY was probably drawn in part from his own life. The
setting was his own Kentucky, and the hero a boy from the
farm who had made his fortune in New York. The scenario
describes how the successful wanderer returns home to rescue his poverty-stricken family, and shows the hero flashing
his hundred-dollar bills and their effect on the natives.
Much of the film was given over to the portrayal of back-
woods life and the narrow attitudes of the Southern revivalist
church. Lillian Gish's role as the quaint country girl who
waits faithfully at home for the return of her lover was one
she was to repeat in TRUE HEART SUSIE. Although begun before THE GREATEST THING IN LIFE, this film was delayed in
production until after its opening. No prints are known to
exist today.

THE GREATEST THING IN LIFE

Opened in Los Angeles, December 16, 1918, and at the
Strand, New York, December 22, 1918. 7 reels.
Scenario by Capt. Victor Marier (D. W. Griffith and S. E. V.
Taylor).
Cast:
Jeanette Peret *Lillian Gish*
Edward Livingston *Robert Harron*
Leo Peret, Jeanette's father *Adolphe Lestina*
M. Le Bébé *David Butler*
The American Soldier *Elmo Lincoln*
The German Officer *Edward Piel*
Jeanette's Aunt *Kate Bruce*
Mlle. Peaches *Peaches Jackson*

Lillian Gish insists that this lost film was one of the best
Griffith ever did. It included one scene which is frequently
cited as proof Griffith did not want to promote race hatred:
the white soldier and the Negro soldier take refuge in the
same shell hole, and the white man kisses the dying Negro

above: *Lillian Gish may be seen in the center of this scene
from* A ROMANCE OF HAPPY VALLEY, *1919.*

opposite left: *Lillian Gish and Robert Harron in* THE GREAT-
EST THING IN LIFE, *1918. (Photo courtesy of The George
Eastman House.)*

opposite right: THE GIRL WHO STAYED AT HOME, *1919. Robert Harron learns he is to be drafted.*

on the cheek. This was more than a passing incident; it was the point of the story. Robert Harron played the role of an intolerant snob, who is unworthy of the heroine, Lillian Gish, but whose prejudices are broken down by the comradeship of the trenches. "The greatest thing in life" is, of course, love. It was a daring theme for 1918, and it is the more remarkable that it came from a Southerner.

A live prologue that Griffith produced for the showing of the film at Clune's Auditorium in Los Angeles included in its cast two young dancers who were destined for leading roles in Griffith films, Clarine (billed as Claire) Seymour and Carol Dempster—and one Mr. Rodolfo Di Valantina, who was also playing roles in the Dorothy Gish series and who became better known as Rudolph Valentino.

THE GIRL WHO STAYED AT HOME
Opened at the Strand, New York, March 23, 1919. 7 reels.
Scenario by S. E. V. Taylor.
Cast:
Monsieur France *Adolphe Lestina*
Mlle. Acoline France *Carol Dempster*
Ralph Gray *Richard Barthelmess*
James Gray *Robert Harron*
Count de Brissac *Syndeconde*
Mr. Edward Gray *George Fawcett*
Mrs. Edward Gray *Kate Bruce*
Herr Turnverein *Edward Reel*
Cutie Beautiful *Clarine Seymour*
A Man About Town *Tully Marshall*
Johann August Kant *David Butler*

This earliest of Griffith's Artcraft films to survive was the last in his war series, and used extra HEARTS OF THE WORLD footage in several exciting battle scenes. While THE GREATEST THING IN LIFE was described in company records as the "official government war picture," THE GIRL WHO STAYED AT HOME also appears to be part of the government's effort to popularize the selective draft amendment. Scenes were shot in the House of Representatives, at local California draft boards and in training camps, and Secretary of War Baker, Provost Marshall Crowder and other dignitaries posed for the camera. By the time such official footage was incorporated into THE GIRL WHO STAYED AT HOME, however, the Armistice had been signed, and no mention was made of any government connection.

To enlist in the campaign for a lasting peace, Griffith included a "good German," in the face of continuing anti-German feeling, first showing him as he leaves a gray-haired mother at home. As the good Johann August Kant, David Butler rouses himself on his deathbed to enjoin a German officer who threatens Carol Dempster with rape to "Fight men—not women"—shooting the officer when his admonition goes unheeded.

Carol Dempster, who was to play the heroine in most of Griffith's later films, replaces Lillian Gish for the first time as leading lady, but neither she nor Richard Barthelmess were required to act very much in THE GIRL WHO STAYED AT HOME, and the limelight is stolen by young Bobby Harron playing a secondary role. As "The Oily Peril," a college-educated lounge lizard with a "killing stance" (it seems

to be based on a stomach cramp), Harron is utterly charming. Drafted despite his father's efforts to have him declared essential in the home shipyards, he is transformed to manhood by a few weeks in an army training camp, and goes on to become a hero on the fields of France. (Ironically, Harron was exempted from the draft by Griffith's intervention. The reason: to make official war pictures.) A nice touch was the stubborn Confederate (Adolphe Lestina) who goes to live in France rather than capitulate to the North, but who finally reacts to the sufferings of the war around him by lowering his treasured Confederate flag in favor of the stars and stripes.

TRUE HEART SUSIE

Opened at the Strand, New York, June 1, 1919. 6 reels. Scenario by Marion Fremont.
Cast:
True Heart Susie *Lillian Gish*
William *Robert Harron*
William's Father *Wilbur Higby*
Susie's Aunt *Loyola O'Connor*
The Stranger *George Fawcett*
Bettina *Clarine Seymour*
Bettina's Aunt *Kate Bruce*
Bettina's Chum *Carol Dempster*
Sporty Malone *Raymond Cannon*

Griffith was so busy with other projects that it is difficult to imagine how he found time to direct the last two or three films needed to fulfill his Artcraft contract. Although the last films were made very quickly, the charming TRUE HEART SUSIE represents Griffith at his most characteristic. Once again he tells a simple story of a small village in rural America, relating it with uncomplicated technique and unobtrusive camera movement and editing. Close-ups are infrequent, most often showing Lillian Gish's lovely and sensitive face. TRUE HEART SUSIE was released so shortly before BROKEN BLOSSOMS that the star's performance in the earlier film was totally eclipsed. Her skillful acting makes the sentimental story genuinely moving, however, and as the naive but faithful Susie, she grows in stature from a funny, happy adolescent to a dignified woman. Only at the end is her characterization marred when in response to Harron's proposal she reverts to the cuteness of an adolescent. Of all Griffith's leading women, Lillian Gish alone could have risen above the cloying sweetness of the role.

Griffith's bitter, defensive sense of humor appears in the titles when he refers to his young lovers as "simple idiots," but it is his sincerity that finally dominates this minor but lovely pastoral study of America before the Jazz Age and the dilemma of the "nice girl" in a small social circle who may have to marry the wrong man or become an old maid.

Although the Artcraft films were simple and inexpensive, they were well made, and the two that survive rate with Griffith's best work. It is a fervent hope of Griffith's admirers that prints of the remaining, lost Artcraft films will yet come to light.

above: *Lillian Gish in* TRUE HEART SUSIE, *1919.*

left: *Childhood sweethearts: Lillian Gish and Robert Harron in* TRUE HEART SUSIE. *(Photos courtesy of The George Eastman House.)*

SCARLET DAYS

Opened at the Rivoli, New York, November 10, 1919.
7 reels.
Scenario by S. E. V. Taylor.
Cast:
Alvarez, a bandit *Richard Barthelmess*
Lady Fair, an Eastern girl *Carol Dempster*
Chiquita, a Mexican dance hall girl *Clarine Seymour*
Randolph, a Virginia gentleman *Ralph Graves*
Rosie Nell *Eugenie Besserer*
The Sheriff *George Fawcett*
Bagley, the dance hall proprietor *Walter Long*

For the last of his Artcraft films, Griffith made a Western, his first since old Biograph days. He described it to Zukor as "a big drama with lots of comedy, real scenery, big action." The story, based on the period of the California Gold Rush, was shot in part on location in Toulumne County during July 1919. According to contemporary reviews, Griffith made an impressive production in this tried and true American genre. Richard Barthelmess played a good-bad-man role that was based to a slight extent on the life of a real "Robin Hood" bandit named Joaquin Murietta. No prints of SCARLET DAYS are known to exist today.

A letter written by S. E. V. Taylor in December 1919 in response to a claim of plagiarism casts an interesting light on how Griffith's scripts were prepared.

"About a year ago, Mr. Griffith told me he wanted a Western story, but made no suggestions about plot, locale or characters. Two weeks later . . . I outlined the plot I had conceived verbally to him. . . . This plot was the same as that presented on the screen with these exceptions. The locale was not California, but Arizona, the time was not 1849, but 1875. . . . Later, when Mr. Griffith began to prepare for his production, the location and time of the story was changed, the bandit was altered to assume the aspects of Joaquin Murietta and three or four historical incidents dealing with this bandit's life were introduced. . . . If he [the studio scenarist] made any suggestions about Murietta and early California these came from his own mind and were the result of his study of and interest in the history of early California. . . ."

Walter Long in SCARLET DAYS, *1919.*

Griffith started production of BROKEN BLOSSOMS in November 1918 between THE GREATEST THING IN LIFE and THE GIRL WHO STAYED AT HOME. Its importance grew in his mind, however, until he withdrew it from the series of program pictures with the idea of releasing it as one of what he called his "specials" or "big pictures"—despite the fact that he was uncertain of whether there was more money to be made from programmers or in the expensive productions for which he was famous.[13]

In January 1919 Griffith joined Douglas Fairbanks, Mary Pickford and Charles Chaplin to form the United Artists Corporation.[14] Although their talents were then the most valuable in Hollywood, their move reflected a fear that realignment within the movie industry might yet limit their potential earnings. However, with the exception of Fairbanks, none of the partners was free to start production. Griffith had to deliver more pictures to Artcraft, and Chaplin and Mary Pickford were tied by contract to First National, which was fast swallowing up the best of Hollywood talent. "The big four," as they were known, were also in need of working capital. To help finance his films for the new company Griffith signed a contract for three pictures with First National on January 21, 1919—only a few days after the formation of United Artists was announced.

Before making the pictures for First National Griffith opened his own Repertory Season in New York, beginning in May with BROKEN BLOSSOMS and following with THE FALL OF BABYLON, the revised and shortened version of HEARTS OF THE WORLD and THE MOTHER AND THE LAW. The season, which ended in August 1919, added much to the Griffith prestige, but little to the Griffith coffers. Griffith subsequently consented to product-starved United Artists' handling general distribution of BROKEN BLOSSOMS, after settling with Adolph Zukor, who had advanced money for it. Thus BROKEN BLOSSOMS became Griffith's first contribution to United Artists in the fall of 1919. Eventually United Artists took over distribution of his other repertory films as well.

It was during the same period that Griffith built his own studio at Mamaroneck, New York, and in the fall of 1919 he moved his entire company there to begin his First National productions. To cope with the vast expense of these enterprises he formed the D. W. Griffith Corporation in 1920. Unlike his earlier business organizations—the David W. Griffith Corporation, which he formed in 1913, and the D. W. G. Corporation, which he formed in 1916—the new company was a public corporation with Griffith its employee and Griffith, his studio and his productions its assets. In trying to free himself from industry control, Griffith had tied himself to investment bankers. Never after was he able to free himself from these new obligations which influenced his decisions for the rest of his career.

BROKEN BLOSSOMS

Opened at the George M. Cohan Theatre, New York, May 13, 1919. 6 reels.

Directed and written by D. W. Griffith, based on "The Chink and the Child," in Thomas Burke's *Limehouse Nights;* photographed by G. W. Bitzer; special effects by Hendrick Sartov;[15] technical advisor, Moon Kwan; music arranged by Louis F. Gottschalk and Griffith.

Cast:

Lucy, the Girl *Lillian Gish*
The Yellow Man *Richard Barthelmess*
Battling Burrows *Donald Crisp*
His Manager *Arthur Howard*
Evil Eye *Edward Peil*
The Spying One *George Beranger*
A Prize Fighter *Norman Selby ("Kid McCoy")*

The following notes supplement Miss Barry's comments on pages 28–29.

With BROKEN BLOSSOMS Griffith proved himself once more the leader of the film world, and the critical acclaim that greeted this film surpassed any he had previously received. Although production costs totaled a modest $88,000, it was necessary to pay Adolph Zukor $250,000 to free the film for United Artists distribution. Nevertheless, BROKEN BLOSSOMS earned a profit—over $700,000 by 1934.

The chief contribution that BROKEN BLOSSOMS made to the art of the film was its poetic atmosphere—the rendition of London fogs, the lights and shadows, the tinted stock in soft blues, oranges and golds, the grays and browns, the lovely soft-focus photography. Perhaps it was these pictorial qualities that Griffith had in mind in later years when he told Ezra Goodman: "What the modern movie lacks is beauty—the beauty of moving wind in the trees. . . ."

BROKEN BLOSSOMS is a controlled film in every respect. Abetted by the influx of German films in the next few years, it had the effect of turning American film-makers away from location shooting. In it Griffith demonstrated that it was possible to recreate an exotic atmosphere within the studio walls although ironically he would have preferred to make the film in London. In fact, Griffith had tried to make a second film in England ever since the summer of 1917, and he never gave up hope that Lord Beaverbrook would provide backing for such a project. His chance finally came in 1935 when he was invited to England to direct the remake of BROKEN BLOSSOMS starring Emlyn Williams, but he left after early casting disagreements, and the film was made without him. Rodney Ackland's *The Celluloid Mistress* (1954) has a fascinating first-hand account of this episode.

Interlude: the films made for First National Pictures

In June 1919, on the way back to Hollywood from his New York Repertory Season, Griffith stopped in Columbus, Ohio, to make arrangements for filming the Methodist Centenary Pageant for the use of the Methodist Church. He dedicated the film that resulted, THE WORLD AT COLUMBUS, to the memory of his mother, who had died in December 1915.

Back in California, he completed the shooting of SCARLET DAYS, which would conclude his Artcraft contract. Even as he edited the last Artcraft film, he started production for First National—anxious for money to build his Mamaroneck studio—and with shooting nearly complete on THE GREATEST QUESTION, he began work on THE IDOL DANCER. As an aide explained when, requesting advances from First National on the second film before the first was completed, "Mr. Griffith works this way." In October 1919 Griffith moved his company, props and costumes to the unfinished Mamaroneck studio—where he prepared SCARLET DAYS for its November 10 opening and shot scenes to complete THE GREATEST QUESTION before departing on November 17 with a small company to do location shooting for THE IDOL DANCER and THE LOVE FLOWER in the Caribbean.

THE GREATEST QUESTION

Opened at the Strand, New York, December 28, 1919. 6 reels.
Directed by D. W. Griffith; story by William Hale, scenario by S. E. V. Taylor; photography by G. W. Bitzer.
Cast:
Nellie Jarvis, "Little Miss Yes'm" *Lillian Gish*
Jimmie Hilton *Robert Harron*
John Hilton *Ralph Graves*
Mrs. Hilton, the mother *Eugenie Besserer*
Mr. Hilton, the father *George Fawcett*
Zeke *Tom Wilson*
Mrs. Cain *Josephine Crowell*
Martin Cain *George Nicholls*

Promoted as a study of spiritualism, THE GREATEST QUESTION pays scant attention to this then popular subject. A mother has a vision in which her soldier son is dying, and at his actual graveside the son reappears and promises his parents another meeting after death. But aside from these novel scenes THE GREATEST QUESTION is the usual melodramatic Griffith story, with love and luck triumphing over villainy. Griffith's First National films were all hastily made potboilers and one suspects much of them to be the work of not very competent assistants. THE GREATEST QUESTION was probably best of the three because Griffith dealt with a subject he knew, rural America, while the next two were set in the exotic tropics of literary convention. However, it compares unfavorably with the earlier rural TRUE HEART SUSIE,

which had a more believable plot and, perhaps significantly, Lillian Gish has forgotten filming any of it despite her generally excellent recall of days with Griffith. The film's best feature is its use of landscape. BROKEN BLOSSOMS' success had not altogether convinced Griffith that films were best shot in the studio. He continued to make use of natural surroundings when his stories allowed, and THE GREATEST QUESTION was shot in California. Griffith told First National on September 5, 1919:

". . . It is also necessary that I take some of the first picture in the east . . . it is really finished now, according to the way they call a picture finished, but nowadays there is so much reshaping, retaking, and re-editing that it will be some little time before it is in final shape. . . ."

The poorest part of THE GREATEST QUESTION is the fast-moving final reel, in which Lillian Gish resists rape and Bobby Harron comes to her rescue. Here again rapid crosscutting is used to increase suspense but this time the tense episode seems gratuitous, the motions mechanical. Ludicrously, after escaping from the would-be rapist, the innocent heroine confides to her sweetheart, "We don't know enough to get married."

THE IDOL DANCER

Opened at the Strand, New York, March 21, 1920. 7 reels.
Directed by D. W. Griffith; scenario by Gordon Ray Young; photographed by G. W. Bitzer.
Cast:
The Beachcomber *Richard Barthelmess*
White Almond Flower *Clarine Seymour*
Walter Kincaid *Creighton Hale*
Rev. Franklin Blythe *George MacQuarrie*
Mrs. Blythe *Kate Bruce*
Peter, a native minister *Porter Strong*
Pansy *Florence Short*
The Blackbirder *Anders Randolf*
Chief Wando *Walter James*

Griffith's adventures while on location for his two other First National films are more exciting than the films themselves. He and his party left New York for Florida in November 1919, and began shooting in Fort Lauderdale. On December 10 he sailed for Nassau on a yacht named *The Grey Duck* with the mayor of Fort Lauderdale aboard as well as his entire staff. Although the trip should have taken twelve hours, it was three days before the party arrived at its destination. In the meantime headlines across the nation reported Griffith as missing, the U. S. Navy was called into action, and airplanes and private ships joined in a hectic search. According to the story, *The Grey Duck* had simply put into a quiet bay on the lee side of Whale Key to avoid a tropical storm, but a few sceptics questioned his story. Whether the incident was actually a publicity stunt has never been determined. An "official" account of the story appeared in Robert Edgar Long's *David Wark Griffith*, which was privately published by the Griffith organization in 1920, but correspondence between Griffith's East and West Coast offices at the time of the incident makes no mention at all of it.

Immediately upon his return from Florida on New Year's Day 1920, Griffith became involved with the production of WAY DOWN EAST, and his interest in completing the First National films was probably no more than perfunctory. Earlier, he had described his plans for THE IDOL DANCER with some enthusiasm. "The second picture," he wrote in September 1919, "which I have already bought from a magazine writer is, I consider, a sure-fire big picture, with lots of action and new environment." Magazine fiction it certainly is. In her first big role Clarine Seymour played a half-breed, "blood of vivacious France, inscrutable Java and languorous Samoa" mingled in her veins, untamed by the missionary civilization on her island, yet not accepted by the natives. Richard Barthelmess was more believable as a drunken beachcomber who is redeemed by love for her. A sickly New England visitor, the nephew of the resident missionary, proves himself a man before he dies in a rousing Griffith climax, with the village attacked by savages, houses set on fire and the virtue of women threatened.

THE IDOL DANCER was Clarine Seymour's last opportunity for fame. Scheduled for the part of Kate Brewster in WAY DOWN EAST, she died after an emergency operation in the spring of 1920.

THE LOVE FLOWER

Opened at the Strand, New York, August 22, 1920. 7 reels.
Directed by D. W. Griffith; based on the story "The Black Beach" by Ralph Stock; photographed by G. W. Bitzer.
Cast:
Stella Bevan *Carol Dempster*
Bruce Sanders *Richard Barthelmess*
Stella's Father *George MacQuarrie*
Matthew Crane *Anders Randolf*
Mrs. Bevan *Florence Short*
The Visitor *Crauford Kent*
Bevan's Old Servant *Adolph Lestina*
Crane's Assistants *William James, Jack Manning*

Although First National announced the release of THE LOVE FLOWER for May 15, 1920, Griffith withheld the film from them after giving a preview to the American Newspaper Publishers Association in New York on April 2 where he gave a speech on his favorite topic, anticensorship. Apparently dissatisfied with it, he then bought the film from First National and arranged for United Artists distribution after shooting additional scenes of Carol Dempster diving.

THE LOVE FLOWER comes off a little better than THE IDOL DANCER. The plot is less complicated, fewer characters are involved in it, and more use is made of the beautiful locations. Richard Barthelmess, wandering the seas on his sailboat, discovers on a South Sea island a young girl (Carol Dempster) who lives alone with her father, a fugitive from the law. Their idyllic romance is interrupted when Barthelmess unknowingly brings to the island the man who is looking for the father. The childlike heroine, supposedly raised on the island, was a type Griffith could create more convincingly than sophisticated sirens. All three of the films Griffith made for First National received some poor reviews, but they were soon forgotten in the wave of excitement that engulfed WAY DOWN EAST.

Kate Bruce greets Griffith on his safe return after being lost at sea, 1919.

Carol Dempster in THE LOVE FLOWER, *1920.*

Independence achieved:
the films made for United Artists

In addition to BROKEN BLOSSOMS and THE LOVE FLOWER, Griffith initiated a third film for United Artists. ROMANCE (1920), which was directed by Chet Withey at the Mamaroneck studio, was a remake of a popular play that Griffith had persuaded the United Artists partners to invest in after having signed it and its star, Doris Keane. ROMANCE lost money for United Artists so that Griffith's first three contributions to the company added little to its coffers. But his next film, WAY DOWN EAST, was to be second only to THE BIRTH OF A NATION as a money-maker.

Before beginning work on WAY DOWN EAST Griffith had planned a series of Bobby Harron films in the manner of the Dorothy Gish comedy series—to be produced under his supervision but without the Griffith name. The first of the series—COINCIDENCE, directed by Chet Withey, was near completion in the summer of 1920 when tragedy struck the company again. On the eve of the New York opening of WAY DOWN EAST, Bobby Harron shot himself in a New York hotel (ominously enough it was the Hotel Seymour), dying a few days later. Griffith's famous heroines tend to overshadow the boyish Bobby Harron. Beginning as an office boy at Biograph, he had stayed on with Griffith and was developing into a very fine actor at the time of his death.

WAY DOWN EAST

Previewed in Middletown and Kingston, New York, during August 1920; opened at the 44th Street Theatre, New York, September 3, 1920. 13 reels.

Directed by D. W. Griffith; scenario by Anthony Paul Kelly from the stage play by Lottie Blair Parker; photographed by G. W. Bitzer and Hendrick Sartov; technical direction by Frank Wortman; art direction by Charles O. Seessel and Clifford Pember; music arranged by Louis Silvers and William F. Peters.

Cast:

Anna Moore *Lillian Gish*
Her Mother *Mrs. David Landau*
Mrs. Tremont *Josephine Bernard*
Diana Tremont *Mrs. Morgan Belmont*
Her Sister *Patricia Fruen*
The Eccentric Aunt *Florence Short*
Lennox Sanderson *Lowell Sherman*
Squire Bartlett *Burr McIntosh*
Mrs. Bartlett *Kate Bruce*
David Bartlett *Richard Barthelmess*
Martha Perkins *Vivia Ogden*
Seth Holcomb *Porter Strong*
Reuben Whipple *George Neville*
Hi Holler *Edgar Nelson*
Kate Brewster *Mary Hay*
Professor Sterling *Creighton Hale*
Maria Poole *Emily Fitzroy*

The fiddler and many of the dancers in the country dance scenes were native Vermonters.

The following notes supplement Miss Barry's comments on pages 30–31.

WAY DOWN EAST, which was planned as a program picture for United Artists, proved so successful that Griffith insisted on road-showing it independently before turning it over to United Artists for the second runs—an arrangement that increased his earnings but irritated his partners considerably.

At the end of March 1920 Elmer Clifton was directing the last of the ice scenes on the Connecticut River with doubles and dummies, and Griffith was back in New York recovering from slight injuries incurred while dynamite charges were being set off to break up the ice jams. The ice was going out in the spring thaw and time was of the essence. Leigh Smith, an assistant, telegraphed Griffith on April 3, 1920:

"Mr. Clifton proved himself a hero today. Allan Law went yellow. Clifton doubled for Law on the moving ice in the middle of the Connecticut River and was rescued by being raised to a bridge by ropes. Hope Clifton's work shows on screen. Knew Clifton would say nothing himself so am sending this wire."

The modest Clifton telegraphed the same day without mentioning the episode. Such was the devotion Mr. Griffith inspired in everyone who worked for him.

Shooting a scene for WAY DOWN EAST, *1920: Griffith seated below camera.*

opposite: *Richard Barthelmess rescues Lillian Gish in the famed ice scenes of* WAY DOWN EAST.

Monte Blue saves Lillian Gish from the guillotine in OR-
PHANS OF THE STORM, *1921.*

DREAM STREET

Opened at the Central Theatre, New York, April 12, 1921. 10 reels.
Directed by D. W. Griffith; scenario by Roy Sinclair (D. W. Griffith), based on two stories by Thomas Burke, "Gina of Chinatown" and "The Lamp in the Window"; music arranged by Louis Silvers.
Cast:
Gypsy Fair *Carol Dempster*
Spike McFadden *Ralph Graves*
Billy McFadden *Charles Emmett Mack*
Sway Wan *Edward Peil*
Gypsy's Father *W. J. Ferguson*
Samuel Jones *Porter Strong*
Tom Chudder *George Neville*
Police Inspector *Charles Slattery*
A Preacher of the Streets *Tyrone Power*
The Masked Violinist *Morgan Wallace*

Although DREAM STREET represents a low point in Griffith's work it comes too early in his career to be considered the beginning of decline, and it is better to think of it as an ambitious but isolated experiment that failed. His intentions with DREAM STREET are clear enough. Returning to the Thomas Burke stories that served him so well for BROKEN BLOSSOMS, he tried to make a second film that would be sheer poetry. While characters are drawn from the real life of the London slums, realism is not the intent, and they are actually depicted as puppets who are pulled through the melodramatic turns of the plot by the forces of Good and Evil personified by a street preacher (the senior Tyrone Power) and a masked violinist (Morgan Wallace, who twice lifts his mask to reveal make-up worthy of Frankenstein's monster). The cast was not up to this difficult blend of melodrama, allegory and poetry.

The contrasts with BROKEN BLOSSOMS are very strange. In the earlier film a gentle Chinese boy selflessly adores the delicate white Lillian Gish; in DREAM STREET an evil Chinese lusts after Carol Dempster, who returns his offer of marriage by betraying him to the police, saying "After this, you let white girls alone."

Except for shots of the London street fog, there is little of the atmospheric photography that contributed so much to the poetic mood of BROKEN BLOSSOMS. Instead there are several of the allegorical scenes that Griffith favored—visions of heaven and of hell and one of the crucifixion—that amount to self-parody. He did introduce an interesting new way of handling his titles, however. Part of the title appears, then another line fades in, and then another in a time pattern that approximates the rhythm of spoken poetry. Had Griffith been a better poet the device could have been very effective.

After a four-week run at the Central Theatre, Griffith moved DREAM STREET to Town Hall, then newly renovated to show movies, and experimented there with synchronized sound—several years before Warner Brothers produced their first sound shorts. The process Griffith tested, developed by Orlando Kellum, involved records that were synchronized with the picture by means of a device attached to the projector. Griffith made records for several of the DREAM STREET scenes but, displeased with the results, limited public performances to a love song by Ralph Graves. Before the feature Griffith himself appeared on the screen and talked optimistically about "The Evolution of Motion Pictures," but his sound experiment was unsatisfactory—both the recording techniques and the synchronization were imperfect—and he did not repeat its use after the Town Hall run.

ORPHANS OF THE STORM

Opened in Boston, December 28, 1921; opened at the Apollo Theatre, New York, January 2, 1922. 12 reels.
Directed by D. W. Griffith; based on the play *The Two Orphans* by Adolph D. Ennery; photographed by Hendrick Sartov; technical direction by Frank Wortman; set design by Edward Scholl; music arranged by Louis F. Gottschalk and William F. Peters.
Cast:
Henriette Girard *Lillian Gish*
Louise *Dorothy Gish*
The Chevalier de Vaudry *Joseph Schildkraut*
The Count de Linieres *Frank Losee*
The Marquise de Praille *Catherine Emmett*
Mother Frochard *Lucille La Verne*
Jacques Frochard *Morgan Wallace*
Pierre Frochard *Sheldon Lewis*
Picard *Frank Puglia*
Jacques Forget-Not *Creighton Hale*
Danton *Monte Blue*
Robespierre *Sidney Herbert*
King Louis XVI *Leo Kolmer*
The Doctor *Adolph Lestina*
Sister Genevieve *Kate Bruce*

Determined to launch another historical spectacle, Griffith had acquired *The Two Orphans,* a popular old-fashioned play in which Kate Claxton had toured for years, transplanting the creaky melodrama within the French Revolution so that actual events could provide a convincing background and the opportunity for spectacle as well. Perhaps Griffith was trying to show himself the master of Ernst Lubitsch, whose MADAME DU BARRY, set in the French Revolution, had aroused such enthusiasm in American audiences in December 1920. The film that resulted, ORPHANS OF THE STORM,

Lillian and Dorothy Gish in ORPHANS OF THE STORM.

was even more expensively produced than WAY DOWN EAST. Fourteen acres of sets reproducing eighteenth-century Paris arose on the Mamaroneck peninsula, giving rise to both publicity stories and active sightseeing.

Throughout ORPHANS OF THE STORM Griffith's film sense is so strong that one is never conscious of its stage origin. The first half is crammed with incident: a murder, kidnappings, orgies, duels, last-minute escapes and finally a pathetic scene in which Lillian Gish hears the adopted blind sister she has been searching for singing in the streets—a scene so powerful that spectators later thought they had actually heard the girl sing.

The second half of the film, originally played after a five-minute intermission, rises to even greater magnificence as it portrays the Revolution itself. The streaming mobs are as frightening as the Klan ride in THE BIRTH OF A NATION, and the storming of the Bastille, the masses surging into streets and squares, with torches and weapons held aloft, must be counted with Griffith's best work. (In several shots he masks the top and bottom of the screen, anticipating the wide-screen ratio, to heighten the dramatic effect.) An unforgettable sequence shows the distraught Lillian Gish caught up against her will by the lawless dancing mob, and the end parallels the famous rescue scene in the modern story of INTOLERANCE, with Lillian Gish about to be guillotined and Monte Blue, as Danton, racing to her rescue with a pardon. Griffith's weaknesses are evident in the bumbling comic touches and the treacly personal story, but the suspense he creates is so great the spectator cannot but be caught up by the orphans' incredible misfortunes.

Reviews were favorable, and ORPHANS OF THE STORM did good business but not good enough. Heavy exploitation costs and road show losses forced the picture into the red even though the income from general distribution was almost as great as from that of WAY DOWN EAST. Significantly, the huge profits of the latter came primarily from road shows, so that Griffith can hardly be blamed for trying to road-show subsequent productions. Poor management, especially on the part of his brother Albert, was probably largely to blame for the losses the road shows incurred, but with the neighborhood movie house established as a normal part of American life big showings in legitimate theatres were no longer the most practical way to sell movies.

Problems with the play rights also added to the expense of ORPHANS OF THE STORM. William Fox, who knew what Griffith was up to, had bought foreign rights from the author's heirs, and held up the London showing of the film with an injunction. Griffith had to settle with him for $85,000 to show the film outside the United States. Taking advantage of the huge publicity that surrounded any Griffith project, an Italian film based on *The Two Orphans* was circulated in advance of ORPHANS OF THE STORM. Another version, from Germany, rested secure in the Griffith vaults to prevent distribution, but in order to avoid confusion Griffith had changed the name of his film from TWO ORPHANS to ORPHANS OF THE STORM after the publicity had been released.

ONE EXCITING NIGHT

Previewed in Connecticut, September 12, 1922; opened in Newport on October 2, 1922; at the Apollo Theatre, New York, October 23, 1922. 11 reels.
Directed by D. W. Griffith; scenario by Irene Sinclair (D. W. Griffith); photographed by Hendrick Sartov; set design by Charles M. Kirk; special effects by Edward Scholl; music arranged by Albert Pesce.
Cast:
Agnes Harrington *Carol Dempster*
John Fairfax *Henry Hull*
Romeo Washington *Porter Strong*
J. Wilson Rockmaine *Morgan Wallace*
The Neighbor *C. H. Croker-King*
Mrs. Harrington *Margaret Dale*
The Detective *Frank Sheridan*
Samuel Jones *Frank Wunderlee*
Colored Maid *Irma Harrison*
The Butler *Percy Carr*
A Guest *Charles Emmett Mack*
Auntie Fairfax *Grace Griswold*
Clary Johnson *Herbert Sutch*

Griffith considered several new enterprises after ORPHANS OF THE STORM, including a film devoted to the history of the world for promoting the League of Nations, and took a hurried trip to London in the spring of 1922 to negotiate for the ambitious project. This film, which was to have had a script by H. G. Wells, never came to fruition. Instead, Griffith began work on ONE EXCITING NIGHT, which he saw as nothing more than an entertaining programmer. Nevertheless, ONE EXCITING NIGHT made a minor contribution to film history. Drawing from early serials, dime novels and the current Broadway successes *The Bat* and *The Cat and the Canary,* Griffith fashioned his film into a murder-mystery thriller, and he hired Henry Hull from the stage version of *The Cat and the Canary* for a major role. He had, in fact considered buying *The Bat,* but wrote his own story under the strange pseudonym of Irene Sinclair, "a young Kentucky authoress," to save money, and his lawyers had to check carefully to be sure that what he had borrowed from *The Bat* was common literary property. In order to copyright his story, he printed and published a few copies of a roughly sketched continuity, from which he departed as soon as he began to shoot.

For what may have been the first time the movie audience was cautioned not to reveal the solution. In fact the plot is so involved and the characters so mysterious that some spectators were not sure that they had understood it. To add to the obscurity, Griffith cut out more and more footage after each preview because the film moved too slowly. But there is plenty of suspense and fright: a haunted house, sliding walls, clutching hands, characters that are not what they seem—and a smashing climax that was brought into the film by an act of nature. On June 11, 1922, a hurricane struck Mamaroneck, and Griffith's cameramen took full advantage of it. One company official explained to another that this was to be "what the ice scene was to WAY DOWN EAST," but the effort to combine the authentic shots with the studio scenes that the plot necessitated resulted in some fake-looking effects.

Today the weakest aspect of the film is its comedy, although it was originally billed as "A Comedy Drama of Mystery," and Porter Strong was widely applauded for his performance as a stock comedy Negro who is terrified by ghosts and night noises. (The same character appears in both THE GREATEST QUESTION and DREAM STREET for, while we now cringe at such racial clichés, it has been only a short time since the figure was common to film, stage and literature.) Strong, a white man, played many blackface roles for Griffith, using make-up that was derived from the ever-popular minstrel shows. Like the country at large, Griffith did not see the minstrel make-up as insulting to the Negro; in fact, he mixed Negroes and blackface white men in the same casts freely, apparently unable to see the make-up as a detriment to realism.

Once again, the film would have made a handsome profit if not for very heavy road show losses. However, it lost less money than any other of the Griffith films of this period.

THE WHITE ROSE

Opened at the Lyric Theatre, New York, May 21, 1923. 10 reels.

Directed by D. W. Griffith; scenario by Irene Sinclair (D. W. Griffith); photographed by G. W. Bitzer, Hendrick Sartov, Hal Sintzenich; set design by Charles M. Kirk; special effects by Edward Scholl; music by Joseph Carl Breil.

Cast:
Bessie Williams, "Teazie" *Mae Marsh*
Marie Carrington *Carol Dempster*
Joseph Beaugarde *Ivor Novello*
John White *Neil Hamilton*
"Auntie" Easter *Lucille La Verne*
"Apollo" *Porter Strong*
Cigar Stand Girl *Jane Thomas*
An Aunt *Kate Bruce*
A Man of the World *Erville Alderson*
The Bishop *Herbert Sutch*
The Landlord *Joseph Burke*
The Landlady *Mary Foy*
Guest at Inn *Charles Emmett Mack*

When ORPHANS OF THE STORM fell short of the financial success he had hoped for, Griffith announced that he was leaving spectacle behind him. Significantly, the program for the first showing of THE WHITE ROSE observes that "One or two human beings could be far more interesting than a thousand remote persons carrying unfamiliar spears." To make this highly pictorial production Griffith went on location during February and March of 1923 in the Bayou Teche country of Louisiana, filming scenes between the towns of Franklin and St. Martinsville, and staying at the beautiful mansion owned by Weeks Hall in New Iberia. Interiors were shot in the rented Hialeah Studios near Miami, Florida.

Weeks Hall was one of the few friends Griffith found time to write to on nonbusiness matters. In a rare reflective mood, while working on a later film, he wrote him:

"I do not think that the picture we made did amount to very much. Some of the best things in it emanated from the atmosphere where the moss hung along the Bayou Teche."

The original print with its toned stock and occasional hand-tinting is gone, and the prints that remain must lack much of its pictorial quality. But enough remains to evoke the beauty of the landscape—the romantic live oaks, the hanging moss and the quiet waters.

THE WHITE ROSE contains the familiar Southern rural scenes of Griffith's boyhood, and they are as successful as ever. But when he attempts to portray the Jazz Age he fails. THE WHITE ROSE looks older than it is. Even the camera setups are unusually prosaic for Griffith. Only the quaint story with its episodes echoing former masterpieces, its excess of sentiment and coincidence, and touches like the drooping rose that symbolizes seduction remind us this is a Griffith film.

The casting of Mae Marsh as "Teazie" represented a long-desired reunion for Griffith, who had been considering how he might use her ever since she had been stolen away from Triangle by Samuel Goldwyn. During a 1921 revival of THE BIRTH OF A NATION Griffith, who had not looked at the film in its entirety for many years, wired her:

"Just saw the greatest performance ever seen on any screen . . . that of the little sister played by Miss Mae Marsh . . . never realized before how good it is meaning your performance."

Her performance in THE WHITE ROSE justifies Griffith's beliefs. Without him her career had declined, but here she again proves herself capable of a moving performance. The exaggerated hip waggling that Griffith undoubtedly introduced for comic effect resulted in clumsy overacting from the bit players. Mae Marsh's exaggerations are more successful in that she isn't a real jazz-baby but only tries to be one, and when she later suffers for it she evokes genuine pathos. The same cannot be said for Ivor Novello, who was imported from England for the role of the fallen minister; though spiritual-looking, his torment is not believable, and as a hero he is a milksop. The rest of the cast is equally inadequate.

The back of the DREAM STREET pressbook in the Griffith Collection contains clippings from 1922–23 about ministers accused of criminal acts, and they indicate how frequently clergymen have been involved in crimes related to sex. Griffith had long been considering a story about a minister who falls from grace but he was worried about church reaction. He consulted with churchmen before beginning production, and later held private screenings for ministers to get opinions for promotional use. To some extent his hesitancy proved to be justified. Not only did ministerial associations object to the film, but in some areas it was banned altogether because the heroine had an illegitimate child (a consideration which apparently did not disturb the viewers of WAY DOWN EAST). More tolerant churchmen realized that Griffith's story taught a moral lesson in keeping with the times, however, and the feeling that a woman alone should suffer—and not the man with whom she had sinned—was by no means universal.

For a brief period the prospects of the Griffith Company looked rosy. The treasurer reported debts being paid from pictures in distribution so that the expected revenue from THE WHITE ROSE would be free and clear. But this happy state of affairs did not last, and once again road show losses eliminated any profit that THE WHITE ROSE might have made.[16]

D. W. Griffith directing Mae Marsh in a scene for THE WHITE ROSE.

Ivor Novello and Carol Dempster in THE WHITE ROSE, *1923.*

AMERICA

Opened at the 44th Street Theatre, New York, February 21, 1924. 12 reels.

Directed by D. W. Griffith; scenario by John Pell from a story by Robert Chambers; photographed by G. W. Bitzer, Hendrick Sartov, Marcel Le Picard, Hal Sintzenich; art direction by Charles M. Kirk; music arranged by Joseph Carl Breil.

Cast:

Nathan Holden *Neil Hamilton*
Justice Montague *Erville Alderson*
Miss Nancy Montague *Carol Dempster*
Charles Philip Edward Montague *Charles Emmett Mack*
Samuel Adams *Lee Beggs*
John Hancock *John Dunton*
King George III *Arthur Donaldson*
William Pitt *Charles Bennett*
Lord Chamberlain *Dowling Clark*
Thomas Jefferson *Frank Walsh*
Patrick Henry *Frank McGlynn, Jr.*
George Washington *Arthur Dewey*
Richard Henry Lee *P. R. Scammon*
Captain Walter Butler *Lionel Barrymore*
Sir Ashley Montague *Sidney Deane*
General Gage *W. W. Jones*
Captain Montour *E. Roseman*
Chief of Senecas, Hikatoo *Harry Semels*
Paul Revere *Harry O'Neill*
John Parker, Captain of Minute Men *H. Van Bousen*
Major Pitcairn *Hugh Baird*
Jonas Parker *James Milaidy*
Colonel Prescott *H. Koser*
Major General Warren *Michael Donovan*
Captain Hare *Louis Wolheim*
Chief of Mohawks, Joseph Brant *Riley Hatch*
Marquis de Lafayette *H. Paul Doucet*
Edmund Burke *W. Rising*
Personal Servant of Miss Montague *Daniel Carney*
Household Servant at Ashley Court *E. Scanlon*
Lord North *Emil Hoch*
A Refugee Mother *Lucille La Verne*
Major Strong *Edwin Holland*
An Old Patriot *Milton Noble*

When Griffith set out to film the Civil War for THE BIRTH OF A NATION, he did it alone and in secrecy. Only his closest staff members knew the magnitude of the production he had in mind, and they were constantly astonished as the vision grew before their eyes. AMERICA, which involved the filming of the Revolutionary War, was made in the full glare of publicity and with the help of historians and historical societies. Griffith welcomed the cooperation of such bodies as the Daughters of the American Revolution because of the promotional value, and through their efforts AMERICA was seen as an ideal vehicle to teach school children about their heritage and the winning of freedom from oppression. As a

young man Griffith had strong personal feelings about "The War Between the States." His views on the birth of his country were less emotional and, atypically, he stayed close to the book written for him by the historian-novelist Robert Chambers. The result was a stodgy film with characters that seem like textbook illustrations.

Griffith had not lost his skill. The enormous battle scenes enlivened with vignettes of action are magnificently filmed. Large numbers of army troops were made available for him to deploy over original battlefields, and prestige put historic buildings and artifacts at his command. As an historic record AMERICA is unsurpassed. As a spectacle it is often thrilling, with a last-minute ride to the rescue that has been edited with all the familiar excitement.

The personal story with which Griffith hoped to set off the larger, historic events was the least effective part of the film. Neil Hamilton as Nathan Holden and Carol Dempster as Nancy Montague lack the spark which would involve the spectator in their affairs, and their scenes together tend to drag. Griffith's personal interest in Miss Dempster may have affected his judgment, and she is especially at a loss in this film.

Lionel Barrymore made a fine villainous Captain Butler. The treatment of this character probably reflects Griffith's anglophilia in that Butler as an individual—and not the British—is seen as the real enemy. However, allowance must be made for the fact that the best surviving print, the one shown by The Museum of Modern Art Film Library, is the English version titled LOVE AND SACRIFICE. The original American version did not stress Butler's American birth, nor did it emphasize that he was hated by the British or call the dispute a Civil War, pitting brother against brother and English-

man against Englishman. Despite such changes LOVE AND SACRIFICE was not destined to be popular in England. Griffith may have made them with an eye to the fate of Robert Goldstein, one of the original investors in THE BIRTH OF A NATION, who had released a film called THE SPIRIT OF '76 just as America entered World War I, and who spent several years in prison when the film was judged unfriendly to our allies.

AMERICA divides into two parts. In the first an endeavor is made to sketch the background of the Revolution from Virginia to New England. The rest of the film concerns the Mohawk Valley campaign and concentrates on the brutalities of the evil Butler. Experts found fault with Griffith's history and his emphasis on the individual villain was criticized. But if, of necessity, he omitted some events, he points to the record for the authenticity of those he included.

No one could find fault with his beautiful handling of the historic battles of Lexington and Concord. The camera placements, editing and rhythmic pace of these superbly express the surge of a people marching for freedom.

After years of distribution, reissue and sale of stock footage AMERICA earned back its cost, but it never was very profitable—possibly because its historical detail and educational spirit were at odds with the Jazz Age in which it was produced.

above: *The "Ride of Paul Revere" (Harry O'Neill) in* AMERICA, *1924.*

opposite: *D. W. Griffith and Colonel Hamilton Hawkins discuss the filming of Morgan's Rangers, played by the Third U. S. Cavalry, for* AMERICA. *Major (later General) Jonathan M. Wainwright, standing by, led the troop.*

Independence lost: ISN'T LIFE WONDERFUL

As Griffith's quarrels with his United Artists partners became more serious, rumors of a split began to spread. To counteract them the partners issued a signed press statement on March 28, 1924, in which they claimed that all were renewing their United Artists contracts and that the company would continue in amity. Griffith viewed this statement as meaningless window dressing and, in secrecy, he signed a contract to make films for Paramount with his old friend Adolph Zukor. While he was abroad making ISN'T LIFE WONDERFUL (partly financed by Zukor) Zukor issued a press announcement on this arrangement, which understandably angered Griffith's United Artists colleagues. To settle his obligation to them, Griffith not only gave United Artists distribution rights to ISN'T LIFE WONDERFUL but also to SALLY OF THE SAWDUST, though the latter was made for Paramount Pictures at its Long Island studio.

What his partners and the general public did not know was the desperate condition of Griffith's finances. A financial statement dated November 1, 1926, reveals that of the United Artists releases from THE LOVE FLOWER through ISN'T LIFE WONDERFUL all except WAY DOWN EAST represented a loss. WAY DOWN EAST was so profitable that the aggregate profit comes to over a million dollars, but this was not enough to offset the heavy expenses of a fully equipped studio and a huge staff. Griffith had to get rid of them and a horde of hangers-on as well. As the property of a publicly owned corporation his bank credit was no longer good, and his United Artists stock was committed to securing bank loans. The $6000 weekly salary he received from Paramount all went to pay off his company debts. The situation was covered up by publicity statements which listed production cost and income of Griffith's films but omitted the exploitation and road show expenses that sent them into the red. Nevertheless, other financial statements dating to the end of 1924 show that Griffith's films as a whole earned more for United Artists than those of any other artist. No wonder they were reluctant to let him go.

opposite left: *The homeless refugees in* ISN'T LIFE WONDERFUL, *1924.*

opposite right: *Hans von Schlettow, Paul Rehkopf and Robert Scholz are the hungry workers who steal the potatoes from Neil Hamilton and Carol Dempster, in* ISN'T LIFE WONDERFUL.

ISN'T LIFE WONDERFUL

Premier at Town Hall, New York, December 4, 1924; opened at the Rivoli Theatre, New York, December 5, 1924. 9 reels.
Directed by D. W. Griffith; scenario by D. W. Griffith, based on a short story by Major Geoffrey Moss; photographed by Hendrick Sartov and Hal Sintzenich; music arranged by Cesare Sodero and Louis Silvers.
Cast:
Inga *Carol Dempster*
Hans, son of the professor *Neil Hamilton*
Grandmother *Helen Lowell*
The Professor *Erville Alderson*
The Brother *Frank Puglia*
The Aunt *Marcia Harris*
Rudolph *Lupino Lane*
Hungry Workers *Hans von Schlettow, Paul Rehkopf, Robert Scholz*
The American *Walter Plimmer, Jr.*

Griffith's flair for melodrama, spectacle, romance and sentiment tends to overshadow the documentary side of his work. There are traces of this documentary aspect in the London slums of BROKEN BLOSSOMS and the modern story of INTOLERANCE but we have to go back to Biograph films like THE MUSKETEERS OF PIG ALLEY to find the purest examples. In ISN'T LIFE WONDERFUL, his story is based on reality, and he used the locations where the actual events occurred with the people who lived there serving as extras. Genuinely inspired by his subject, Griffith approached it with a renewed surge of creativity, and made one of his best films.

It is probable that the subject matter of ISN'T LIFE WONDERFUL, the deprivations of the defeated Germans, was suggested to Griffith by J. C. Epping. This lifelong associate, who had been his trusted advisor on fiscal matters since 1914, was a German citizen, with relatives in Germany. What he saw and reported to Griffith after a visit there in 1922 must have inspired ISN'T LIFE WONDERFUL, although Moss, the author of the short story on which ISN'T LIFE WONDERFUL is based had witnessed the same conditions. Griffith collected what information he could before leaving for Germany with his company, and during July and August 1924 he shot the film on location: the street scenes in Old Berlin, the forests in Crampnitz and Sacrow, the shipyard at Copenick, the potato patch in Grunaw.

Concerned about the lingering effects of anti-German propaganda, he changed the poor family in the story to a group of Polish refugees living near Berlin, but he makes clear that it is a story of human beings everywhere who have been debased by the evils of war. Despite the question of American reception Erich Pommer advised Griffith that the film would not go in Germany; even if the effect was pro-

German in America, he felt that the Germans themselves would still be likely to regard ISN'T LIFE WONDERFUL as an attack.

It is a common fault in Griffith's work that the characters lack subtlety, appearing as either entirely good or completely evil. However in ISN'T LIFE WONDERFUL, even the villains of the piece are ordinary working men who have been driven to crime by hunger, and when Inga calls them beasts, they reply: "Yes, beasts we are, beasts they have made us." Griffith's professional players act with unusual restraint. Carol Dempster, with her hair pulled back and in shabby clothes, gains a stature she never achieved in any of her other films.

Griffith shows keen observation in such sequences as the one in which the family sits dully at their dinner of turnips. Hunger and malnutrition, breadlines and riots are portrayed with stark realism, and the muted grays of the photography contribute to the somber effect. If the film occasionally lapses into sentimentality, it is redeemed by the climactic sequence in which the potatoes are stolen. Here is a chase unlike any other Griffith chase. There are no contrived effects, and the suspense is not pushed beyond belief. In a beautifuly staged and photographed sequence, the two lovers hurry through the tall trees as darkness approaches with their precious store of potatoes, pursued by the desperate workers who at last overtake and rob them. The picture ought to have ended with the two lovers trying to console one another, but Griffith tacked on a happier ending, "a year later," which detracts from it. Miss Barry (page 32) has mentioned the lasting influence of this film on subsequent film-making, and we can easily compare it with the neorealism of post-World War II Italian films. For Griffith it was to be the last great film, after which he gave up his long-fought-for independence and went to work as an employee of Adolph Zukor.

Wage slavery: the films made for Paramount Pictures

SALLY OF THE SAWDUST

Opened at the Strand, New York, August 2, 1925. 10 reels.

Directed by D. W. Griffith; scenario by Forrest Halsey, based on the play *Poppy* by Dorothy Donnelly; photographed by Harry Fischbeck and Hal Sintzenich.

(Produced under Paramount contract, but distributed by United Artists, see page 74.)

Cast:
Sally *Carol Dempster*
Professor Eustace McGargle *W. C. Fields*
Payton Lennox *Alfred Lunt*
Mrs. Foster *Effie Shannon*
Judge Foster *Erville Alderson*
Leon, the acrobat *Glenn Anders*
Mr. Lennox, Sr. *Charles Hammond*
The Detective *Roy Applegate*
Miss Vinton *Florence Fair*
The Society Leader *Marie Shotwell*

It must have been difficult indeed for the great David Wark Griffith to submit to a major studio operation where he could no longer have the staff that he had trained and where he would have the story decisions, budgets, and casting imposed upon him by the studio heads. It is not surprising that the films he made for Paramount were not up to his earlier standard, but it would be unfair to blame all their shortcomings on the system. At first Paramount executives were willing to defer to Griffith as the acknowledged leader of the film world. He, however, had begun to lose confidence; although badly in need of restoring his reputation as a money-maker, he did not know how to go about it.

SALLY OF THE SAWDUST was a film that Griffith himself suggested to Paramount. His box office sense was still good, and although comedy was not his strong point, he was aware of its current popularity. Somehow he had the imagination to let W. C. Fields have his head, and while Fields had appeared in one or two previous movies it was this film that assured his success as a film star. For the first time audiences met the fully-developed character of Fields the debonair rapscallion, the con man with a tender heart. Much of Fields' business in SALLY OF THE SAWDUST—his sleight of hand, his finesse with a cigar ash, his aplomb in the face of adversity—must have come from the play on which the film was based, for he had already achieved Broadway success in the same role. But his ride on the bucking, runaway Ford is pure movie, and a deliriously funny sequence. The more sentimental parts of the story needed a slick, light touch in order to carry the implausible plot. Slickness was a quality Griffith never acquired, however, and beside Fields' delicate savoir-faire, the other parts of the film seem clumsy. Some of the best scenes—the traveling troupe, the boarding house, the

riding in boxcars—came from Griffith's own youthful barnstorming days, and perhaps it was that aspect of the play that originally appealed to him.

THAT ROYLE GIRL

Opened at the Strand, New York, January 10, 1926. 11 reels.

Directed by D. W. Griffith; scenario by Paul Schofield, from the serial and novel by Edwin Balmer; photographed by Harry Fischbeck and Hal Sintzenich.

Cast:
The Royle Girl *Carol Dempster*
Calvin Clarke, Deputy District Attorney *James Kirkwood*
George Baretta *Paul Everton*
The Royle Girl's Father *W. C. Fields*
King of Jazz *Harrison Ford*
and *Florence Auer, Marie Chambers, George Rigas, Ida Waterman, Alice Laidley, Frank Allworth*

Reluctant to keep their highly paid director in idleness, Paramount executives rushed Griffith into production of another W. C. Fields film even before SALLY OF THE SAWDUST was completed. Griffith objected violently to the script, which had been at the Paramount studio for years and which had been discarded by other directors, but Jesse Lasky urged him to work with it.[17]

Fields played only a minor comedy part in THAT ROYLE GIRL. The story centered around a girl of the Chicago slums who holds to the ideals represented by Abraham Lincoln while moving through the Chicago underworld, the world of jazz and a term in jail. According to a contemporary account in *The New Yorker*, Carol Dempster, "having become a 'manikin,' is being shown the bed by her songwriting seducer. The bed fades out and into the statue of Lincoln, whom Miss Royle holds as an ideal. The incumbent [*sic*] seducer loses out."

THAT ROYLE GIRL was originally seen as a "small" picture, but studio executives subsequently decided that the film needed more punch. To rescue Miss Dempster from her seducer, a second *deus ex machina* in the form of a $100,000 cyclone was added to the Lincoln statue, and Griffith went far over budget. Whether the resulting film bore any trace of his work we do not know, since no prints are known to exist today.

THE SORROWS OF SATAN

Opened at the George M. Cohan Theatre, New York, October 12, 1926. 9 reels.

Directed by D. W. Griffith; scenario by Forrest Halsey, adaptation by John Russell and George Hull; from the novel by Marie Corelli; photographed by Harry Fischbeck; edited and titled by Julian Johnson; art direction by Charles Kirk; miniatures by Fred Waller.

Cast:

Prince Lucio de Rimanez *Adolphe Menjou*
Geoffrey Tempest *Ricardo Cortez*
Princess Olga *Lya de Putti*
Mavis Claire *Carol Dempster*
Amiel *Ivan Lebedeff*
The Landlady *Marcia Harris*
Lord Elton *Lawrence D'Orsay*
Dancing Girl *Nellie Savage*
Mavis' Chum *Dorothy Hughes*

Although THE SORROWS OF SATAN was bought by Paramount for Cecil B. De Mille, the latter wrote in his autobiography that no De Mille production was included in Paramount's November 1924 announcement of forthcoming releases because negotiations to buy Marie Corelli's novel had not yet been completed. De Mille's disagreements with Paramount must have been the real reason for the omission. As early as September 1924 Griffith mentioned *his* plans to make the film, and he later claimed that the project had been forced on him.[18] Paramount had obviously foreseen Zukor's acquisition as a potential replacement for its mainstay, De Mille, who left to form his own company by the end of the year.

above: *Lya de Putti in* SORROWS OF SATAN, *1926.*

left: *W. C. Fields plays the old shell game in* SALLY OF THE SAWDUST, *1925.*

THE SORROWS OF SATAN, postponed until after Griffith had made SALLY OF THE SAWDUST and THAT ROYLE GIRL, was planned as a big and expensive production. The financial disaster that resulted marked the end of Griffith's long relationship with Zukor. In what must have been one of his lowest moments Griffith wrote Zukor a ten-page letter recapitulating the difficulties he had encountered in the course of trying to fulfill his contract. The letter makes clear that conflicting instructions from Zukor, Lasky and other executives made a shambles of the budget and the picture, but the saddest element is its revelation of Griffith's loss of confidence.

Advance publicity led the public to expect spectacle from THE SORROWS OF SATAN, but at Zukor's insistence it became more love story than anything else and the endless close-ups of the lovers, Ricardo Cortez and Carol Dempster, that dominate the first half-hour of the film strike an early note of dullness. The orgy scene, reduced by Paramount's editor to a few shots of barefoot nymphs chased by satyrs, caused laughter even then. Even miniatures, costing in the neighborhood of $55,000, were given to Fred Waller to do over Griffith's objections. At last the entire film was taken from Griffith for re-editing by Julian Johnson, and changes Griffith did not approve were made in the story sequence. Zukor, who had seen the earlier version but not the final one, was displeased with the changes and, unreasonably, blamed Griffith for permitting them. The arguments that ensued were bitter.

Griffith himself can hardly be criticized for his lack of interest in the warmed-over De Mille project. The only parts in keeping with his own inclination were the scenes emphasizing the romance of poverty—and the lovers in the rooming house, without money for rent, food and coal, might have been drawn from his own youth with Linda Arvidson, when he too had struggled to become a writer.

Return to Hollywood:
the films made for Art Cinema Corporation

It is sometimes assumed that when Griffith went back to United Artists in 1927 he returned to independence. Nothing could be further from the truth—for his financial position utterly prevented him from producing independently. Paramount had paid off the Griffith Company's most urgent debts as the price of buying up Griffith's contract; but since they owned all the films Griffith had made for them, he had no recent films to use as collateral.

When United Artists was founded Harry Abrams, its most active executive, was primarily involved in selling films to exhibitors. When Abrams died in 1926 Joseph Schenck, who had come in two years earlier as production head, be-

above: *Lionel Barrymore discovers the adulterous lovers, Mary Philbin and Don Alvarado, in a scene from* DRUMS OF LOVE, 1928. *(Photo courtesy of The George Eastman House.)*

opposite: DRUMS OF LOVE: *Don Alvarado in center.*

78

came the real controlling force in United Artists affairs. Schenck had his own stable of film-makers, including Norma Talmadge (his wife) and Buster Keaton (his brother-in-law), and he was responsible for attracting many other important artists. Earlier, United Artists had been product-starved, the original partners sometimes contributing no more than one big production a year. It was Schenck who put the company on its feet by initiating sufficient output to support the enormous system of exchanges that Harry Abrams had set up.

Anxious to bring Griffith back, Schenck offered to finance his productions through his own Art Cinema Corporation (which distributed through United Artists). In exchange, he requested script approval, the privilege of voting Griffith's United Artists stock, and several similar details which added up to Griffith working for him as he had for Zukor. Griffith finally signed with Schenck on April 19, 1927, but not before he had seriously considered an offer to join Cecil B. De Mille's Producers Distributing Company, which was affiliated with Pathé and the Keith-Albee theatre circuit. Alarmed at this latter prospect, Griffith's advisors had urged him to accept the United Artists offer. In this case their advice was well-founded, and not long after the De Mille effort failed.

Returning to Hollywood for the first time since 1919, Griffith found the movie industry greatly changed and the production studio system infinitely more complicated. While he and Schenck tried to come to an agreement on the story for his first film, he took on one small interim assignment. One of Schenck's current productions, TOPSY AND EVA, directed by Del Lord, did not satisfy him, and he asked Griffith to take over. Anonymously, Griffith shot some additional scenes and recut the film. Schenck announced himself pleased with the results.

DRUMS OF LOVE

Opened at the Liberty Theatre, New York, January 24, 1928. 9 reels.
Directed by D. W. Griffith; scenario and titles by Gerrit J. Lloyd; photographed by G. W. Bitzer, Karl Struss, Harry Jackson.
Cast:
Princess Emanuella *Mary Philbin*
Duke Cathos De Alvia *Lionel Barrymore*
Count Leonardo De Alvia *Don Alvarado*
The Court Jester, Bopi *Tully Marshall*
Duchess De Alvia *Eugenie Besserer*
Duke of Granada *Charles Hill Mailes*
Maid *Rosemary Cooper*
The Little Sister *Joyce Coad*

It seems likely that Griffith fastened on a sex theme for his next film with one eye on the box office. His basic reasoning was sound enough, but somehow he and Schenck mis-

calculated when they lit upon this particular story of Paolo and Francesca transposed to nineteenth-century Latin America. DRUMS OF LOVE is frankly a story of sexual passion. Inasmuch as it involves adultery, however, it could in 1927 only end in tragedy—and Griffith and Schenck both should have known that tragedy was not good box office. In an effort to rectify their error Griffith shot a new, happy ending after the film had been shown, but within the context of the original legend it is ludicrous, and exhibitors liked it no better than the first tragic one. In it the court jester-spy kills the husband and leaves the lovers alive to atone for their sin, kneeling before a crucifix, candles flickering before their faces. Both endings survive.

There is little in this film to mark it as Griffith's. Some stirring and beautifully executed battle scenes in the early part are similar to those in THE BIRTH OF A NATION, but they have little to do with the story. After them the film settles down to interminable close-ups of the principals, lovely in themselves but, since Don Alvarado (a fourth-string Latin lover in the Valentino tradition) and Mary Philbin have not more than two facial expressions apiece, the close-ups are a mockery of the old Griffith style. From time to time expensively produced glass shots are inserted—for no apparent reason other than to break up the lengthy indoor scenes. The titles—by Gerrit Lloyd, one-time publicity man for Griffith, now inexplicably turned to for scripts—are incredible.

Even though her introductory appearance shows her as an innocent child with her cat, the character played by Mary Philbin is a far cry from the typical Griffith heroine, and she is quickly identified as more the seducer than the seduced. The camera movements that describe her consciousness of her own sexual appeal are very skillful and show Griffith as less prudish than usual. It is Lionel Barrymore, however, stuffed out with pillows to become the hunchback monster with a tender heart, whose performance is the film's saving grace. His glances over Mary Philbin's head and the cigar that he holds behind her back as he embraces her while mentally preparing to go to war are superb touches.

Griffith's increasing cynicism is evident in a letter he wrote in March 1928 instructing his office staff to eliminate scenes for the censors but then to slip them back, on the theory they would not be noticed. His concern with censorship increased as he tried to recover his popularity with sex themes, but wiser heads at United Artists prevailed, and he was not permitted to carry through his plans for cheating.

THE BATTLE OF THE SEXES

Opened at United Artists Theatre, Los Angeles, in September 1928; opened at the Rialto, New York, October 12, 1928. 10 reels.

Directed by D. W. Griffith; scenario by Gerrit Lloyd, based on the novel by Daniel Carson Goodman, *The Single Standard;* photographed by G. W. Bitzer and Karl Struss; synchronized music by R. Schildkret.

Cast:
Judson *Jean Hersholt*
Marie Skinner *Phyllis Haver*
Mrs. Judson *Belle Bennett*
"Babe" Winsor *Don Alvarado*
Ruth Judson *Sally O'Neil*
Billy Judson *William Bakewell*
Friend of Judsons' *John Batten*

Frankly searching for money-making schemes, Griffith decided to remake his 1913 success THE BATTLE OF THE SEXES. Phyllis Haver was chosen to play the gold digger and Jean Hersholt to be the middle-aged lothario, and Griffith tried to bring the old melodrama up to date by adding touches of comedy to the two characters. (Hersholt's part came midway in his transformation from the villain—as which he had long been typecast—to the kindly old doctor roles for which he became famous.)

Contemporary reviewers had been kind on the whole to DRUMS OF LOVE; for THE BATTLE OF THE SEXES Griffith received the worst of all his reviews. Most critics agreed he would have done better to reissue the original. They deplored the cheap sensationalism and the slow pace of the new version, but at least one of them found amusing the barber shop sequence in which Phyllis Haver first sees Hersholt as a man who might be worth mining.

A synchronous music track with sound effects and a theme song sung by Phyllis Haver were added to this essentially silent film, and it is as a silent film that it survives today. It was typical of this period of Griffith's career that he had little to do with the synchronized score, and that when he heard it he didn't like it. Still floundering, ill at ease in the new Hollywood, his attitude was frequently negative. As at Paramount, he was subject to the advice of too many superiors at Art Cinema Corporation, and he no longer had the strength to fight for his own ideas. People who knew him at the time say that he had begun to drink heavily.

Phyllis Haver in THE BATTLE OF THE SEXES, *1928.*

Jean Hersholt, in THE BATTLE OF THE SEXES, *struggles to regain his youthful figure.*

Lupe Velez in LADY OF THE PAVEMENTS, *1929.*

LADY OF THE PAVEMENTS

Opened at the United Artists Theatre, Los Angeles, January 22, 1929. 9 reels.

Directed by D. W. Griffith; scenario by Sam Taylor, based on a story by Karl Volmoeller; photographed by Karl Struss, assisted by G. W. Bitzer; set design by William Cameron Menzies; synchronized music arranged by Hugo Reisenfeld; theme song by Irving Berlin.

Cast:

Nanon del Rayon *Lupe Velez*
Count Arnim *William Boyd*
Countess des Granges *Jetta Goudal*
Baron Finot *Albert Conti*
Baron Hausemann *George Fawcett*
Papa Pierre *Henry Armetta*
Dancing Master *Franklin Pangborn*
A Pianist *William Bakewell*

Griffith had difficulty in reaching agreement with Joseph Schenck over scripts, and as the failures multiplied Schenck was less and less inclined to trust his judgment. LADY OF THE PAVEMENTS, a Ruritanian romance and Griffith's only attempt in the genre, was to have been made by Sam Taylor, but Schenck assigned the project to Griffith after Taylor had completed a shooting script. Set in the Paris of 1868, it deals with a countess (Jetta Goudal) who having been rejected by her noble fiancé (William Boyd), determines to make him pay for saying that he would rather marry a woman of the streets. She finds a café soubrette (Lupe Velez) and grooms her to pass as a lady of social position, but when the count and the disguised soubrette (inevitably) fall in love

and he learns of her true origins he brings himself to forgive her.

Lupe Velez' personal-appearance tour with LADY OF THE PAVEMENTS was a sensation, but the critics had reservations about her performance in the film. As John S. Cohen, Jr., remarked in *The New York Sun:*

"Mr. Griffith has turned her animalism into cuteness. He has done her hair up into little pompadours, made her pigeon-toed, and rather coy, and when she begins to upset court functions, one is reminded of the gosling days of the Gishes and the Dempsters."

LADY OF THE PAVEMENTS featured an elaborate multiple-exposure scene in which thirteen William Boyds fill a room, then rise and merge into one. To achieve the effect, Ned Mann (who was the fifth special effects man hired to try it) exposed the negative through the camera thirty-six times. Griffith also had some elaborate ideas about the sound in the film, and tried to increase and decrease the volume of Lupe Velez' singing voice as she approached or retreated from the camera. Unfortunately, this proved to be beyond the abilities of his technicians. There was some question whether the poorly synchronized sound that resulted would be recorded on the film "as in the Fox method," but discs won out, and thus the sound for this film is also lost.

ABRAHAM LINCOLN

Opened at the Central Theatre, New York, October 25, 1930. 10 reels.

Directed by D. W. Griffith; scenario by Stephen Vincent Benét; photographed by Karl Struss; set design by William Cameron Menzies; production supervision by John W. Considine, Jr.; music arranged by Hugo Reisenfeld.

Cast:

Abraham Lincoln *Walter Huston*
Ann Rutledge *Una Merkel*
Mary Todd Lincoln *Kay Hammond*
Stephen Douglas *E. Alyn Warren*
General Lee *Hobart Bosworth*
General Grant *Fred Warren*
Colonel Marshall *Henry B. Walthall*
General Sheridan *Frank Campeau*
Sheridan's Aide *Francis Ford*
Midwife *Lucille La Verne*
Tom Lincoln *W. L. Thorne*
Nancy Hanks Lincoln *Helen Freeman*
John Wilkes Booth *Ian Keith*
Stanton *Oscar Apfel*
Offut *Otto Hoffman*
Armstrong *Edgar Deering*

Jetta Goudal in LADY OF THE PAVEMENTS.

82

Lincoln's Employer *Russell Simpson*
Sheriff *Charles Crockett*
Mrs. Edwards *Helen Ware*
Herndon *Jason Robards*
Tad Lincoln *Gordon Thorpe*
John Hay *Cameron Prudhomme*
General Scott *James Bradbury, Sr.*
Young soldier *Jimmy Eagles*
and *Hank Bell, Carl Stockdale, Ralph Lewis, George McQuarrie, Robert Brower*

William de Mille must have been subject to a trick of memory when he wrote in *Hollywood Saga* that Griffith had made a speech before the Academy of Motion Picture Arts and Sciences in 1928 asking the members to officially condemn sound pictures. According to one contemporary newspaper account of the speech Griffith actually welcomed talking pictures.[19] Some of his doubts about sound stemmed from such personal experience as his experiment with a synchronized DREAM STREET, but he continued to be alert to new techniques and inventions that might re-establish him as a pioneer. Throughout his career he investigated color processes, screen ratios, and attachments for the camera, and it was with renewed enthusiasm he began his first "all-talkie."

After much searching and on the brink of a final rupture, Griffith found a film that he and Schenck could agree on. Schenck must have felt discouraged about Griffith's work, and by the summer of 1929 he was avoiding meeting him. Griffith had threatened to quit, but his colleagues in the D. W. Griffith Company who were afraid of the financial consequences urged him to hold on. Finally Schenck consented to an ambitious production of a film devoted to Abraham Lincoln, a subject that lay close to Griffith's heart.

Carl Sandburg, a movie fan as well as a Lincoln expert, offered to write the script for ABRAHAM LINCOLN, but he wanted more than Schenck was willing to pay. Instead, it was Stephen Vincent Benét who was assigned the screenplay and who received film credit for it. Much of Benét's poetic script was discarded, however, in favor of a version that was only partly his with additions by Gerrit Lloyd and Griffith. Later Griffith wrote (in a draft of a letter never mailed to Schenck):

"I am more of the opinion than ever that had we followed the original Benét script of 'Abraham Lincoln' with its subsidiary love story, and not put the name of Lincoln on the marquee, we would have had a success with the people of all classes, and would not have hurt the main story concerning Lincoln. In fact, it would have made a real story instead of connecting episodes. When Lincoln pardons the boy in the tent scene he would have pardoned someone whom we all knew and loved instead of it being merely an episodic incident. It would also have given us some suspense as to what would have happened to at least two of our characters until the very end. The audience already knows what is going to happen to Lincoln. He alone can furnish very little suspense."

In poor health when ABRAHAM LINCOLN was in production, Griffith described it as a "nightmare of the mind and nerves," and departed for a favorite hideout in Mineral Wells, Texas, when the shooting was barely completed. The miniatures and special effects were executed after he left, and the film was edited under the supervision of John Considine, Jr. It was previewed in San Diego and then sent on to New York, where Griffith saw it completed for the first time. After the New York preview showings he wanted (as always) to make changes, but Considine rejected them. Griffith and Schenck agreed to part, forgetting about a fifth picture for which they had contracted. Griffith's parting words were "too many cooks spoil the broth."

Despite these difficulties, ABRAHAM LINCOLN briefly restored Griffith's prestige. Why it was so well received and his next film, THE STRUGGLE, was laughed at can probably

be understood only in the context of the early days of sound —ABRAHAM LINCOLN is not great enough nor THE STRUGGLE bad enough to explain such polar reactions today. Countless static "all-talkies" poured out of Hollywood in 1930. The best directors quickly learned to make use of sound without letting it take over the picture, however, and Griffith was one of them. In his first talkie he made free use of "off-screen" sound effects and voices, moving the camera when he wanted and recording sound later if necessary. Nevertheless, there is less action than we expect in a Griffith film, and many of the outdoor shots look as if they were made in the studio.

As Lincoln, Walter Huston stands above the rest of the cast head and shoulders—both literally and figuratively—expressing emotions with his whole body, his stance and—in a series of moving close-ups—of his face. He provides one of the film's great moments when he reacts to news of Ann Rutledge's imminent death but the film is generally uneven. It contains lyrical passages—the slow pan in the pasture where Lincoln trysts with Ann Rutledge; the sequences in which Northern and Southern soldiers march off to war—and Sheridan's ride to rally his soldiers is executed with verve and style. Other historical scenes are rendered as stilted tableaux, however, and famous quotations are clumsily inserted.

Episodic, the film attempts to encompass the whole of Lincoln's life from birth to death, presenting him as a man of the people with a weakness for funny stories and a love of comfort. Griffith's sincere admiration for his subject is apparent throughout, but we cannot help making detrimental comparisons with his earlier films. The scene of Lincoln's assassination is a poor successor to the moving sequence in THE BIRTH OF A NATION. When the crowd demands a speech from him in his box at the theatre, he obliges by reciting his Second Inaugural Address. In Griffith's defense it should be noted that the words "Again, I say . . ." which were cautiously inserted before the actual speech are not in the shooting script.

Walter Huston plays the title role in ABRAHAM LINCOLN, *1930.*

The last film: THE STRUGGLE

THE STRUGGLE

Opened at the Rivoli, New York, December 10, 1931. 9 reels.
Produced by D. W. Griffith, Inc.; distributed by United Artists; directed by D. W. Griffith; screenplay by Anita Loos and John Emerson; photographed by Joseph Ruttenberg; edited by Barney Rogan; music arranged by Philip Scheib and D. W. Griffith.
Cast:
Jimmie Wilson *Hal Skelly*
Florrie *Zita Johann*
Nina *Charlotte Wynters*
Nan Wilson *Jackson Halliday*
Johnnie Marshall *Evelyn Baldwin*
Mary *Edna Hagan*
Sam *Claude Cooper*
Cohen *Arthur Lipson*
Mr. Craig *Charles Richman*
A Catty Girl *Helen Mack*
A Gigolo *Scott Moore*
A Mill Worker *Dave Manley*

Some quirk of vanity caused Griffith to deduct five years from his age throughout his professional life. At 56, however, he was plainly tired, and he rested for the year following ABRAHAM LINCOLN. He was convinced that his years of failure were the result of working for others with insufficient control of the film-making process, and he was sure that he could achieve success again if he could manage to produce a film on his own in the East. In 1929 the D. W. Griffith Company had been awarded a sizable tax refund (due to a 1920 overpayment), and the company treasurer had invested the money in stocks without telling Griffith. Despite the state of the stock market these investments had proved to be good. By 1931 the company was able to get a small bank loan that was sufficient to activate Griffith's plans, and THE STRUGGLE was made cheaply and hastily in a rented Bronx studio.

It is not easy to understand why THE STRUGGLE was received with such universal disapproval. Audiences laughed at it, and one of the trade papers declined to review it out of respect for Griffith's former greatness. Griffith hid in the seclusion of his hotel room and refused to see anyone. United Artists, which had advanced some of the production costs in exchange for distribution rights, withdrew the film and cut it hastily to attempt wide distribution before word of its failure spread. It never went beyond a few showings in Philadelphia. Some years later it was revived briefly as a "laugh" movie under the title TEN NIGHTS IN A BARROOM.

Although it may have looked more old-fashioned in 1931 than it does at this remove, THE STRUGGLE is certainly not the least of Griffith's films: The addition of dialogue to his typically melodramatic scenes must have shocked audiences as much as the first florid love phrases that John Gilbert spoke aloud. In BROKEN BLOSSOMS the image of Donald Crisp drunkenly abusing a cowering Lillian Gish had been effective; in THE STRUGGLE, the same situation abetted by sound effects and dialogue proved to be ludicrous. Nevertheless, THE STRUGGLE scene is well staged. Hal Skelly gives a convincing performance, and the close-ups of his shattered face are remarkable.[20]

THE STRUGGLE avoids the theatrical dialogue that was common to the early talkies. Griffith tried to capture everyday speech, and his characters are more apt to toss out a casual "Yeah?" than to engage in clever repartee. Unfortunately, his attempted realism fails because the actors were simply not up to his demands. Zita Johann, acquired from the Broadway stage for her first film role, is particularly inadequate.

Why THE STRUGGLE did not have a better script, given old hands like John Emerson and Anita Loos to write, is a puzzle. The sound film demanded more complex motivation, subtlety and depth than could pass on the silent screen, but to all appearances Hal Skelly's motivation for return to drink is that his wife wants him to wear a flowered lavender tie. The message of THE STRUGGLE is muddled, too. Griffith intended to underscore the evils of Prohibition, in particular poisonous bootleg liquor; what came out, however, was a morality play on the evils of drink with a plot that is not much more sophisticated than his 1909 Biograph one-reeler, A DRUNKARD'S REFORMATION.

The film does contain many sharply etched realistic touches—the Bronx street scenes, the splendid factory sequences (made at the Stamford Rolling Mills in Springdale, Connecticut), and the shots of Hal Skelly in the horrors of delirium tremens are all well done. The nostalgic opening sequence in a pre-Prohibition beer garden and its contrasting scene of a twenties jazz café are also effective.

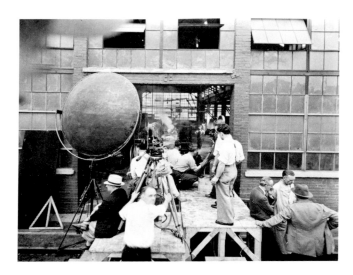

above: *Shooting the scenes in the Stamford Rolling Mills for* THE STRUGGLE, *1931.*

below: *Inside the factory.*

To — Al Hunger,
from — Billy Bitzer.
"With Best Regards"

August 2nd 1931

G. W. Bitzer and D. W. Griffith.

D. W. Griffith lived until July 23, 1948, but he never made another film. For a few years he did make some half-hearted efforts, working on old scripts and negotiating with potential backers. The remake of BROKEN BLOSSOMS has been mentioned earlier (page 60). He also wrote and narrated a radio series (in 1933) in which his reminiscences were fictionalized. In 1939, Hal Roach hired him as "producer" of ONE MILLION B.C., but probably for the publicity value of his name. Griffith's ideas were not wanted, and though he stayed and drew his salary throughout the production, he left, taking his name with him, before the film was released. He returned to his first love, playwriting, and bought plays written by others with the idea of starting a new career as a Broadway producer. But this too came to nothing. He took up golf and riding, drank a lot, and tried to play for the first time in his life.

The D. W. Griffith Company went into receivership after THE STRUGGLE but gradually Griffith recovered. He did not live in poverty. He sold his stock in United Artists to his former partners, and had some good nonmovie investments as well as occasional income from reissues or remakes of his films. He owned ranch property in California, but he never had a real home in his adult life, living always in hotels. He supported improvident brothers, sisters and nephews as he always had, in the Southern tradition of close family ties and responsibilities. In 1936, Griffith married the young actress Evelyn Baldwin, having been separated from Linda Arvidson since 1911. The second marriage was no more lasting than the first.

When The Museum of Modern Art gave the retrospective exhibition of his work that resulted in the first edition of this book in 1940–41, Griffith returned briefly from obscurity. By 1947 he was living alone at the Hollywood Knickerbocker Hotel, forgotten by most of the world and withdrawn from human contact. In *The Fifty-Year Decline of Hollywood* Ezra Goodman gives a mordant portrait of Griffith at this time, hiding in his room, declining to answer mail or telephones. As one of his relatives has observed, he hid his feelings from the world out of an excessive pride that made his later years hellish. He died in his lonely hotel room of a cerebral hemorrhage at the age of 73.

NOTES

1 Griffith's first two-reel film, originally issued in separate parts by Biograph, was reissued as one film July 4, 1916.

2 A two-reeler, issued by Biograph in two parts, was reissued as one film August 29, 1916.

3 Although this film was copyrighted on this date and shown in Europe, it was not released in the United States until February 26, 1914.

4 William K. Everson credits Tony O'Sullivan as the director of this film.

5 Also spelled "Aitken" in some contemporary sources.

6 Later, the Film Library acquired negative and print of the version of THE BIRTH OF A NATION which was issued with a soundtrack in the 1930s. Although much shorter than the silent prints, it contained shots not in them. The Hollywood Museum has since discovered additional print material, and collated all the sources to make as complete a print as possible.

7 While Griffith was in the East supervising the New York opening of INTOLERANCE, he spent a few days in Albany and produced a one-reel film, A DAY WITH GOVERNOR WHITMAN, for use in the Whitman campaign for re-election. No prints of this film are known to exist today.

8 Listed as Georgia Pearce on the original program because of her more important role in the Babylonian story.

9 Listed as Robert Lawler on the original program.

10 The sun was almost the only light source for INTOLERANCE. Even the motif of Lillian Gish rocking the cradle was lighted by a ray of sun coming through a hole in the roof. One of Griffith's subtitles for the film was "A Sun-Play of the Ages."

11 Additional financing came from the War Office Cinematograph Committee in England, which bought future rights for the British Empire. Although he also got the official blessing of the French government, he had to pay $5,000 for the privilege.

12 James and Rose Smith were the cutters on almost all Griffith's films.

13 A far from disinterested advisor, Griffith's brother Albert Gray thought he should make both types of films but disassociate himself from the big companies and assign road-showing to Albert himself.

14 William S. Hart was supposed to join the group but withdrew.

15 Hendrick Sartov who had been signed to a contract as a special effects man in October 1918 assisted Bitzer on this film. Later, he photographed the follow-up film, DREAM STREET.

16 Griffith's next project, a costly failure, involved Al Jolson. Although the story had been paid for and contracts forecast and director signed, Jolson, who was to star, fled precipitately when the first rushes were shown. On June 24, 1923, Griffith received a telegram from the S.S. *Majestic* reading "Ordered by physicians to take ocean voyage immediately owing to my nervous condition. . . ." It was to be several years before Jolson attained movie fame by breaking into speech during the course of THE JAZZ SINGER. The Griffith Company sued him but recovered only $2,627 in damages, and Griffith turned the project over to his brother Albert, who tried to recoup the loss by producing the film as HIS DARKER SELF with Lloyd Hamilton in Al Jolson's blackface role. Griffith would have been wiser to have written it off as a loss at the beginning.

17 It was Lasky who had the task of telling Griffith in October 1926 that his method of producing pictures was not Paramount's, and that Paramount had decided to dispense with his services.

18 The novel from which he worked was also the literary source for Carl Dreyer's LEAVES FROM SATAN'S BOOK; coincidentally, INTOLERANCE was the inspiration for the Dreyer work.

19 What scandalized Academy members was his insistence that "motion pictures is more of a business than an art"; even if many of them secretly agreed, it sounded too cynical when said by the man they supposed to represent Art in motion pictures. Actually, Griffith's feelings about art and business in movies were ambivalent, and his opinion depended on his mood.

front cover, left to right:
Sherman's March to the Sea in THE BIRTH OF A NATION, *1915.*
Blanche Sweet in JUDITH OF BETHULIA, *1914.*
Lillian and Dorothy Gish in AN UNSEEN ENEMY, *1912.*
The climax of the modern story in INTOLERANCE, *1916.*

back cover:
D. W. Griffith